Beyond Boundaries:
Innovation through Openness

Beyond Boundaries: Innovation through Openness
(경계를 넘어; 열린계를 통한 혁신)

First edition, first printing: February 20, 2025
First edition, first publication: February 25, 2025

Author: Yoo Ki-pung (유기풍)
Publisher: Jeon Ik-kyun (전익균)

Composition: Jo Yang-je (조양제), Kim Ki-Chung(김기충), Yoon Jong-Ok(윤종옥)
Marketing: Kim Ji-hye(김지혜), Kwon Tae-hyung(권태형), Kim Jung-Won(김종원)
Proofreading: heo Gang (허강), Jeon Min-Seo (전민서), Kim Hye-Sun(김혜선)
Design: Kim Jung(김정)
Sales/Distribution: Saevit Comms

Publisher: Saevit Publishing Company (도서출판 새빛)
Telephone: 02)2203-1996 Fax: 050)4328-4393
Inquiry about publishing and manuscript submissions, Email: svcoms@naver.com
Website: https://blog.naver.com/svcoms
Registration Number: 215-92-61832 Registration Date: July 12, 2010

Price: 17,500 KR
ISBN 979-11-91517-91-0 (03190)

Saevit is implementing a program to maximize various marketing effects for authors by establishing a single system for publishing, media promotion, and events. Saevit is doing its best to make authors the protagonists of each field.

Beyond
Boundaries:
Innovation through
Openness

Unless we break down the closed boundaries of the system,
we cannot transcend our narrow limitations.
If we want integration and open innovation for ourselves and the organizations
we belong to, we must first open the boundaries of our minds and
thoughts locked in a closed box. Numerous limitations are now erecting walls like a
'closed system' in front of our young people. Do not settle for the narrow world of
a closed dimension! Open the box of your closed mind and move towards
an 'open system', and you will see infinite possibilities and the power of positivity.

Ki-pung Yoo

AEVIT
BOOKS

About the author,
Dr. K. -P. Yoo

Born in Yangju, Gyeonggi, South Korea in 1952, Ki-pung Yoo earned his BS in Chemical Engineering from Korea University in 1977. He subsequently pursued graduate studies in the United States, receiving a Ph.D. in Chemical Engineering with a specialization in statistical thermodynamics from the University of Connecticut, Storrs in 1983.

Returning to Korea in 1984, Dr. Yoo joined the faculty of Sogang University, where he dedicated nearly 35 years to teaching and research in the fields of energy, molecular thermodynamics, and supercritical fluids. In 1990, he was awarded a fellowship from the Alexander von Humboldt Foundation and served as an invited professor at Oldenburg University in Germany. He has also served as a Visiting Professor at Washington State University and Purdue University.

Dr. Yoo held prestigious administrative positions, including the 14th President of Sogang University from 2013 to 2016 and the 4th President of the KEPCO International Nuclear Graduate School (KINGS) in Ulsan, Korea from 2021 to 2024. He is currently an emeritus professor in the School of Engineering at Sogang University.

Dr. Yoo was awarded the Order of Blue Stripe for Service (清操勤政勳章) by the South Korean government in 2022, in recognition of his lifelong dedication to the advancement of higher education.

▮
Foreword

Dear reader, do you find yourself open to the world, or closed off to its possibilities? Do you yearn for a future brimming with hope, shaped by transformative innovation, or are you content to dwell in the familiar comforts of the present?

This book, I assure you, is no mere armchair read. It dares to ask these very questions, and so much more. With an open heart and a curious mind, it embarks on a grand journey across time and cultures, weaving together insights from diverse fields of knowledge - much like the laws of thermodynamics reveal the intricate dance of energy and matter - to uncover fresh pathways to hope.

Penned by a distinguished chemical engineer - a scholar who once explored the intricacies of thermodynamics and later served as president of leading Korean universities with a passion for progress - this work is a testament to a life lived at the vibrant intersection of intellect and action. His experience in these presidencies brings a wealth of knowledge in academic leadership and a deep understanding of the forces that shape our world.

More than a simple treatise, this book offers a beacon of possibility: the 'open system' project. May its wisdom inspire the youth of the 21st century to step forward with courage and embrace a world of open doors, open hearts, and an open future, brimming with promise.

Chan J. Wu (Literary Critic, Loyola Library Director, Sogang University)

Foreword

The author of this book is a professor who taught me thermodynamics in college. I vividly remember struggling with his incredibly difficult, open-ended exam questions about energy. In fact, I must confess that getting a good grade in his class was harder than getting one at Wharton Business School, where I later studied.

Thermodynamics, the only 'physical science' course in our chemical engineering department, was a subject that taught me how nature and humans communicate logically. I remember learning about the properties of matter, energy, entropy, and the evolution of systems.

In this book, the author expands on the concepts of entropy and energy to emphasize the importance of 'open systems'. He argues that open systems, which freely interact with their surroundings, have a higher chance of evolving into a new, positive state, even in extremely unstable situations. It's like how companies must constantly adapt and communicate with the outside world to survive in a rapidly changing market environment.

The author's insights have been a great help to me in making wise decisions amidst the challenges my company has faced. I highly recommend this book to all entrepreneurs who feel lost in this era of uncertainty!

Woo-hyun Lee(Chairman, OCI Holdings, Co., Ltd., Korea)

▮
Foreword

The author emphasizes the importance of an open perspective for both individual and organizational development in today's rapidly changing and complex world. He argues that 'open systems', which are based on this open perspective, must freely exchange resources like materials, energy, goods, and information with the outside world in order to evolve. This, he says, brings positive change to both individuals and organizations.

This book reinforced my belief that our company must strengthen the openness of our technology, talent, and values to achieve our goal of becoming a total IT network solutions provider. An open perspective is no longer limited to academia; it is a crucial philosophy for businesses navigating a competitive landscape. I want to work with young talent who possess this open perspective to further develop our company.

I recommend this book to young people who dream of starting their own businesses and to network solution providers who, like our company, strive to create a healthy and safe internet environment.

Tae Joo Kim(Chairman, Plantynet, Co., Ltd., Korea)

A Colleague's Perspective on the Author

An 'Open System' leader who innovates the university by breaking down closed boundaries

While Dr. Yoo isn't someone you would typically associate with rigid authority, he projects the air of a gentle and scholarly elder. This demeanor shifts when discussing certain subjects like educational reform, social justice, or scientific innovation. He becomes a passionate advocate, bold and free-thinking, with a strong personality that some describe as uncompromising. In a recent faculty meeting, he challenged the status quo by proposing a radical overhaul of the university's core curriculum. This is the person leading Sogang University, an institution often perceived as conservative.

Dr. Yoo has published hundreds of papers, secured billions of won in personal research grants, and earned a reputation as a dedicated mentor who stays up late with his students, helping them write papers. He is a person who never gets tied down and confidently walks his own path, as evidenced by his decision to leave a prestigious position at a national university to return to his alma mater, Sogang. He has supported countless students by providing scholarships. Perhaps this explains his objectivity, and why he is the right person to lead the university into a new era.

As an engineering graduate, President Yoo's genuine pursuit of both practicality and creativity is evident in Sogang University's quiet but significant transformation. Under his leadership, Sogang is charting a new course for universities seeking to redefine themselves in a changing academic landscape. Furthermore, symbolic of this shift, President Yoo sold his official Equus sedan, a luxury car typically associated with high-ranking officials, and now drives a more practical Carnival, a family van. His pursuit of financial independence for the university, reducing reliance on tuition fees, is central to his innovative strategy.

Sogang University, long known for its rigorous academic program, is often compared to Sogang High School, a prestigious high school affiliated with the university and known for its highly competitive entrance exams. President Yoo is also reimagining Sogang High School. Rather than adhering to a traditional, closed, one-way model of education, he envisions a two-way, open approach. Instead of attempting to teach everything, his vision for Sogang's future emphasizes motivating students and encouraging them to actively engage in their own learning.

It is President Yoo who champions this 'open system' project. Although I have known him personally for over 20 years, and this is not the first time I've heard him speak about it, his vision always fills me with excitement. President Yoo's 'open system' is a dynamic proposal. It has the potential to bring about substantial changes and renewal in our lives, from Sogang University to the entire world.

I sincerely hope that this innovative approach will take root and flourish, contributing significantly to the innovation of universities. I believe it can transform our nation and the world, ultimately creating a more vibrant society for all.

Young-ho OH(President of the Korean National Academy of Engineering, Professor at Sogang University), **who passed away in 2023**

CONTENTS Beyond boundaries: Innovation through Openness

Chapter 2

The Application of Open Systems | Open-Minded People, An Open World

Chapter 3

The History of Open Systems | Open Sciences, Open Humanities

Chapter 4

Challenges in Open Systems | Seek and Ye shall find

Chapter 5

Leaders of Open Systems | Forefront Figures of Open Systems

▮

The hearts of a scientist, a poet, and a sculptor are not so different. That's why my emotional dreams have been able to survive intact in a world dominated by facts and verification. What I'm trying to say is that just because someone dreamed of being a poet and then became a scientist, it doesn't mean they've lost their dreams. On the contrary, they've become a rare kind of 'scientist with a poet's heart'.

- From Choi Jae-cheon's "The Scientist's Library" -

Prologue

Open your heart to enable new innovation

- A Proposal for an "Open System" project to advance one more step
  from the top of a hundred-foot pole(百尺竿頭 進一步)

A hundred-foot pole stands tall, an awe-inspiring sight. Some are daunted by its height, while others, filled with determination, ascend again and again until they reach its peak. Standing at the summit, one feels a sense of solemnity. Memories of the hardships endured surface, bringing with them a profound sense of accomplishment and the quiet satisfaction of knowing one has given their all. It's easy to become caught up in the exhilaration of reaching such heights through exceptional effort. However, dwelling in this exhilaration and self-satisfaction can lead to complacency, blinding one to a higher realm or deeper truth.

This is why the ancients wisely advised taking one more step from the summit. While this might seem like a leap into the abyss, it symbolizes a greater rebirth. Throughout history, those who have opened up new realms of understanding, achieved profound enlightenment, or expanded the horizons of human creativity, have embodied this spirit of transcending perceived limitations. This wisdom comes from the Buddhist text "Jingde Chendeng Lu (景德傳燈錄)," written by Dao Yuan of the Song Dynasty, Chinna.

I believe this attitude exemplifies an 'open system,' and I long to share this message with today's youth. Together, I hope we can take a giant leap forward from the peak, embracing the unknown and continually striving for greater understanding and growth.

What is an Open System?

Many might wonder. An open system is a fundamental concept in thermodynamics, a field I studied as an engineer. While I'll delve deeper into the specifics of open systems, and how they differ from closed or isolated systems, in the main text, let's consider this: Our universe is vast, and the world is incredibly complex and interconnected. In this context, an open system is something that freely exchanges matter and energy with its surroundings, regardless of its size or defining boundaries.

Through various engineering research projects, I've come to realize that the concept of an open system extends far beyond thermodynamics, into everyday life and professional work. With this book, I aim to expand and deepen this discussion, bridging the gap between engineering logic and life wisdom.

Simply put, whether we consider an individual or a group, positive evolution, and even innovation or greater change, becomes possible when we maintain an open attitude. By opening our minds, breaking down barriers, and freely communicating and sharing information with the world, we can foster innovation and dynamically open up new horizons of creation.

Nowadays, we hear a lot about convergence and creative fusion. Few would deny their importance. But where and how should we converge and fuse? While the path may seem wide open, I believe an open-system approach is the most essential prerequisite. An open attitude, rather than a closed-minded, egocentric one, provides the foundational strength for convergence, fusion, and open innovation. Expecting these things without an open-system mindset is like building a castle in the air.

I hope that the youth of this era and this land will cultivate the foundational strength for open self-innovation, enabling them to spread their wings and soar. I hope they will freely explore the world, breaking through boundaries with an open-system perspective. That's why I wrote this book—to help them transcend rigid disciplinary boundaries and engage with the world in a truly open way.

Let's pause for a moment and reflect. Have we ever truly aspired to reach the peak of a hundred-foot pole? Have we given up halfway? Once at the peak, have we become complacent, building walls and remaining stagnant? Or have we dared to take a giant leap forward?

Our reflections apply to individuals, organizations, universities, companies, and beyond. Perhaps academic societies or intellectual groups are trapped within self-made, isolated enclosures. Can we truly achieve new academic creations within such confines? Are some organizations resting on their laurels, inviting stagnation and decline? It's time for honest self-reflection. Without breaking down these barriers, there can be no open innovation. Closed individuals become prisoners of their own making. A closed system leads to a closed university, stifling growth and progress.

On the other hand, an open system evolves into an open discipline and an open university, fostering a dynamic environment where knowledge flourishes. Creativity and innovation inherently know no boundaries. It's the thirst for knowledge and the drive for creativity that transcends limitations and changes the world. That is the essence of convergence and fusion. An open system is the path to an open and positive world. This is the starting point of the 'open system' project.

Humanities without natural sciences are ignorant; humanities that ignore science are empty. Why do we pursue science? Why do we build cars or focus on semiconductors? Ultimately, all science is connected to the quality of human life. Science and academics are about discovering new values and creating a better world. If they become detached from humanity and devolve into empty rhetoric, they cannot be called true scholarship.

What are the humanities? They are the study of the quality of our lives. They involve contemplating how we should live in this world and with what values and beliefs. However, it's a misconception to think that the humanities are merely about sensitivity and emotion. Consider philosophy. It's a discipline that challenges our rational judgment, and its depths are not easily plumbed. Yet, the deeper we delve, the more fascinating it becomes. I believe this rational aspect of philosophy shares a kinship with natural science. Perhaps the very essence of philosophy and science is one and the same.

The intersection of philosophy and science is the foundation of an open system and the starting point for convergence and fusion. It is where knowledge transcends disciplinary boundaries and leads to true innovation and a better world.

The Industrial Age demanded well-trained graduates who excelled at following instructions. This model, however, is no longer effective in the 21st century. The IT revolution has dissolved boundaries and democratized information. Consider the rise of MOOCs (Massive Open Online Courses). Which course would attract more students: 'Justice' taught by a little-known junior scholar, or the same subject eloquently delivered by Harvard's renowned Michael Sandel? Or consider the impact of social media, where information is readily available anytime, anywhere.

As we move beyond the 20th-century industrial model and into the 21st-century knowledge-based society, education must evolve. The traditional teacher-centered, standardized approach must give way to a more interactive, two-way pattern, where mentors and tutors guide students toward self-directed learning. Professors should no longer be 'one-man shows' but facilitators who motivate students and cultivate their ability to utilize information effectively.

In this regard, Sogang University aims to be a pioneer. If

traditional education was a one-way '1.0' system centered on the instructor, we are now striving to create a two-way '2.0' system that empowers students and encourages them to take ownership of their learning journey.

High school students often struggle academically after being divided into science and humanities tracks for university admissions. We aim to lead the way in addressing this issue. In the age of the internet and smartphones, universities must open their doors and embrace a new era of learning. Education is no longer confined to the classroom. We must provide open education in an open world. With a few clicks, anyone can access world-class lectures from institutions like Harvard. This is what an open university truly represents.

There's no need to limit job searches to domestic opportunities. People are fundamentally similar everywhere, and countless opportunities exist in every country. We often remain ignorant of these possibilities simply because we lack the courage to explore them. But with a single step outside our comfort zones, a world of infinite possibilities unfolds. 'Knock, and it will be opened to you' is not just an empty saying. Creativity belongs to those who dare. An open system welcomes those who dare to venture beyond the familiar.

Those caught up in relentless competition become trapped in a closed system. Those who seek to escape that competition and discover new values embody the spirit of an open system. The blue ocean—a metaphor for uncontested market space—is the doorbell to an open system. Today's youth, often passively carried along by societal currents, desperately need the empowering spirit of an open system. I want to instill this spirit in our students first and foremost.

The world's innovations often begin with small gaps, those overlooked areas where creativity can flourish. I hope more people will actively seek out these gaps. I hope many young people will courageously enter these spaces and challenge the world's injustices and limitations.

I cordially invite you, young people who dream of an open future, to join the 'open system' project. Together, let us embrace positive evolution and open innovation to create a better world.

My family is a "super-connected" open family, spanning Seoul, LA, and Anchorage. We built our family in the US during the 80s, but later returned to Seoul, while our sons remained. Now, video calls connect us instantly. My granddaughters even attend their

US school virtually while visiting us. It's an amazing open world compared to my time abroad. Love to Chloe, Haley, Scarlett, and Harlow. I hope they too will build open families and become a truly global, "super-super" family.

Originally published in Korean by SAEVIT BOOKS in January 2016, this edition has been partially revised and translated into English by the author in December 2024.

to understanding an open system:

Steve Jobs

the most famous owner of an apple since Isaac Newton

Perhaps South Korea hasn't produced its own Steve Jobs because we diligently focus on a single major, confining ourselves within that field. While specialization has its merits, it can also limit our perspectives and hinder innovation in a rapidly changing world.

Consider Steve Jobs. He wasn't confined to technology or science. Through Pixar, he helped create the world's first 3D animated film, Toy Story, and with iTunes, he revolutionized the way we listen to music, demonstrating a rare ability to blend science and art. Few individuals in our country seamlessly integrate different fields as effectively as he did.

Jobs's success raises an important question: Could Korean scientists readily embrace that same interdisciplinary perspective? The scientists who worked with Steve Jobs placed great importance on design. As I'll explain later, the definition of an open system is complex. But before delving into those complexities, let's consider Steve Jobs, a man who embodied the spirit and constitution of an open system. By examining how he transcended boundaries and integrated different fields, we can understand how truly innovative individuals are nurtured.

M. O. O. C.

**The opening of numerous online open courses
at prestigious universities worldwide.**

The idea of only listening to lectures within a classroom is a closed system. When thoughts are closed, knowledge cannot flow or develop.

In English-speaking countries like the Philippines and India, universities are already on the brink of extinction due to competition with MOOCs. To be blunt, Korea is only surviving because of the language barrier.

Soon, domestic universities will have to compete with world-renowned American universities in terms of "lecture quality." What will we do then? Both students and universities must prepare for open lectures.

MOOCs are the keyword that will be discussed most in this book.

What is a MOOC?

A Massive Open Online Course (MOOC) refers to large-scale, interactive learning that takes place over the web. Unlike traditional classes that use videos, handouts, and workbooks as supplementary materials, MOOCs foster a community among students, professors, and teaching assistants centered around online discussion boards. MOOCs represent an evolution of distance learning.

The term MOOC, which refers to online open courses using the internet, originated in Europe in the early 2000s but experienced rapid growth in the United States around 2010. This surge was fueled by educational companies partnering with prestigious Ivy League universities to provide course content. Renowned institutions such as Stanford University, Princeton University, the University of Pennsylvania, and MIT made their in-house lectures accessible to a vast online audience. Currently, there are over 2,400 courses available worldwide."

The keyword 3 to understanding an open system:

Google

The world's premier destination for creative individuals.

Google is a search tool. But its search function is evolving at a remarkable pace. But Google's ambitions extend far beyond simple web searches. They are increasingly interested in accessing and analyzing a different kind of data: our own biological information.

Through genetic testing services like 23andMe, you can discover where your ancestors lived and determine the percentage of Mongolian and Korean blood in your body. This service was even selected as the Invention of the Year by Time magazine in 2008. Google is not only interested in gathering information about the world but also in our biological data.

Everyone searches. What's truly important is not producing new information, but manipulating existing information in novel ways. Google's open system makes this possible. With a little effort, you too can learn to leverage information and create new possibilities.

Definition of an 'Open System'[1]

What on earth is an open system?

The universe is vast. Within its expanse lies the galaxy, and within the galaxy, our solar system. Earth, one of the planets within this system, is enormous. Yet, we humans are but fleeting specks of dust, inhabiting a tiny space on this vast planet. The universe is infinite in both space and time. However, despite this immensity, all interactions and phenomena among these existences are interconnected in an open state, without restriction.

Thermodynamics, a branch of physical science, explores human interactions with natural phenomena. It is my area of expertise. In this context, 'dialogue' refers to the process of seeking scientific answers to our innate human curiosity about the world around us.

---

1. It should be noted that the content related to the definition of an 'open system' in this section is a reworking of material previously covered in my books and translations, adapted to fit the format of this book.

 - Yoo Ki-pung, Energy and Thermodynamics, Ajin Publishing, 2000.

 - Yoo Ki-pung, Mixtures and Equilibrium Properties, Ajin Publishing, 2001.

 - I. Stengers & I. Prigogine, translated by Yoo Ki-pung, Order out of Chaos, Minumsa, 1998.

How do we approach the complexities of a particular object or the changes-the evolution-of a natural phenomenon?

Here, 'nature' encompasses not only the natural world we inhabit but also the artificial environments created by humans: devices, processes, factories, even groups of people. When we are curious about this 'artificial nature,' we can seek logical answers just as we do when studying the natural world.

The objects of our interest, while diverse, are all interconnected parts of an open universe. To understand how an object evolves over time, we must quantitatively examine the exchanges between the object and its surroundings. This includes analyzing the changes occurring within the object itself. To achieve this, we establish a boundary that distinguishes the object from its environment and carefully observe how the object's properties change.

In physical science, particularly thermodynamics, we often define an object interacting with its surroundings as a 'system.' We then analyze this by dividing it into three components: the system itself, the boundary, and the surroundings. The system's behavior is heavily influenced by the characteristics of its boundary. This method of analysis, known as 'system analysis,' is crucial for understanding how systems evolve.

To understand how a system evolves as it exchanges energy or matter with its surroundings through its boundary, we must first examine the boundary's characteristics. These characteristics can be broadly classified into three types. The most idealized type is an isolated boundary. An isolated boundary prevents any exchange between the system and its surroundings, whether it be material or immaterial.

Consider an open system that freely exchanges heat, matter, or anything else with its surroundings. What happens if this system is suddenly isolated? Imagine that, at the moment of isolation, the temperature, pressure, or concentration of a particular component within the system is unevenly distributed. Interestingly, over time, heat will spontaneously flow from hotter to colder regions, and the component will move from areas of higher concentration to lower concentration. Eventually, these internal differences vanish, and the system reaches a uniform and static state where no further changes occur. This phenomenon, a fundamental principle observed in nature, illustrates a key characteristic of natural evolution—the tendency towards equilibrium.

A system exhibits certain characteristics where various non-uniform factors within it change according to specific principles. When these non-uniformities, often described as potentials, exist within a system, a flux flows from a region of high potential to a region of low potential to offset the difference. This transfer phenomenon, known as the internal relaxation process, continues until the potential difference-the driving force of the flux-disappears.

Importantly, regardless of the type of potential, the change always occurs unidirectionally, towards the dissipation of the potential. Through this internal relaxation process, the system eventually evolves into an equilibrium state. This equilibrium state is completely uniform, where no further internal relaxation processes occur, and no factors inducing change remain.

For a living organism, this state represents death. All living things thrive on the exchange of energy and matter with their surroundings. In a truly isolated state, life ceases. Therefore, changes within a system enclosed by an isolated boundary inevitably leads to a static and ultimately lifeless outcome.

It's important to remember that such an isolated boundary is a highly idealized or abstract condition. In the real world, truly isolated systems do not exist. Everything is interconnected and constantly interacting.

The concept of an isolated boundary is useful when dealing with highly complex systems. It allows us to focus solely on the system itself and observe its changes in the most idealized and simplified manner. However, once a system enclosed by an isolated boundary reaches equilibrium, it effectively "forgets" how it arrived at that state. It cannot spontaneously return to its previous non-equilibrium condition.

To reverse this process and return the system to its previous state requires a significant expenditure of energy. Think of it like descending a mountain. Going downhill is a natural, spontaneous process driven by gravity. Potential energy is dissipated as you descend to a lower altitude. However, climbing back up the mountain requires a considerable effort. You must expend energy to overcome gravity and regain the lost potential energy.

Similarly, in an isolated system, reaching equilibrium is like reaching the bottom of the mountain. To move away from this state and reintroduce non-uniformities requires external intervention and an input of energy.

In physical sciences, the evolutionary characteristics of a system enclosed by an isolated boundary are explained using the concept of entropy. When a non-uniform potential exists within an isolated system, a flux arises, moving in the direction that dissipates this potential difference. This process always leads to an increase in the system's entropy.

Entropy can be understood as a measure of disorder or randomness within a system. As the internal relaxation process proceeds, the entropy function, which is defined as a continuously increasing function, reaches its maximum value when the system reaches equilibrium. In other words, maximum entropy corresponds to a state of equilibrium.

For a system in equilibrium to revert to its initial non-equilibrium state, the entropy of the system would have to decrease. However, this contradicts the second law of thermodynamics, which states that the entropy of an isolated system can only increase over time or remain constant in the case of reversible processes.

The German physicist Rudolf Clausius, one of the founders of thermodynamics, famously used the entropy function to describe the evolution of the universe, assuming that the universe itself is an isolated system. This led to the concept of the 'heat death of the universe,' where all energy is eventually evenly distributed, and no further change is possible.

"Die Entropie der Welt strebt einem Maximum zu"
"The entropy of the world strives towards a maximum."

This statement, known as the Second Law of Thermodynamics,

is a cornerstone of classical thermodynamics. It describes the inevitable increase in entropy within isolated systems and is often referred to as the principle of maximum entropy. However, for this principle to hold true for the universe, a fundamental question must be addressed: is the universe truly isolated?

Evidence suggests that the universe is far more likely to be open rather than isolated. Therefore, applying the Second Law of Thermodynamics to the universe as a whole may be an oversimplification. It represents a highly idealized interpretation of reality. To accurately analyze systems with closed or open boundaries, which allow for the exchange of energy and matter with their surroundings, a new logical framework is needed. This framework must account for the dynamic interactions and exchanges that characterize the universe as we observe it.

Next, we can consider a closed boundary, a condition somewhat less restrictive than the idealized isolated boundary. A closed boundary allows for the exchange of certain physical quantities between the system and its surroundings while preventing others from crossing. In physics, this often refers to a boundary that permits energy transfer but prohibits the exchange of matter.

For example, imagine a system with a temperature difference compared to its surroundings. If the boundary is made of a heat-conducting material, thermal energy will flow from the higher temperature region to the lower temperature region. If the system's temperature is lower, heat will flow out of the system and into the surroundings.

Another example involves a piston-cylinder device. If there is a pressure difference between the system and its surroundings, mechanical energy can be transferred by moving the piston. The piston's movement allows work to be done on or by the system, depending on the pressure gradient. A common example of a closed boundary that facilitates mechanical energy exchange is a stirrer, which transfers energy into the system through the rotating motion of a shaft.

Generally, the evolution of a system within a closed boundary is more complex than in an isolated system, but it shares some key characteristics. While the evolution of an isolated system is governed by the principle of maximum entropy, the evolution of a closed system is guided by the principle of minimum free energy.

Free energy, in this context, represents the energy available within a system to do useful work. As the system evolves and internal potential differences dissipate, it progresses towards a state of equilibrium where free energy is minimized. This minimization of free energy drives the system's evolution.

Depending on the specific characteristics of the closed boundary, different types of free energy are used to describe the system's behavior. If the system's volume is held constant, the Helmholtz free energy, $A = A(T,V,N)$, is used. This function depends on temperature (T), volume (V), and the number of particles (N). If the system's pressure is held constant, the Gibbs free energy, $G = G(T,P,N)$, is used, which depends on temperature, pressure (P), and the number of particles.

Just as an isolated system tends towards maximum entropy, a closed system tends towards minimum free energy. Both principles reflect the natural tendency of systems to evolve towards a state of equilibrium where no further driving forces for change exist.

Finally, we arrive at the most realistic boundary condition: the open boundary. In this case, the system interacts freely with its surroundings, exchanging both matter and energy. This conceptual boundary closely resembles real-world situations, where systems are rarely, if ever, truly isolated or closed.

However, there is currently no single, universally applicable scientific method to explain the evolution of open systems. Their diversity and the complexity of their interactions defy simple explanations based solely on entropy or free energy. Traditional equilibrium thermodynamics, which focuses on closed and isolated systems, falls short when dealing with the dynamic flux and constant exchange characteristic of open systems.

Understanding the evolution of open systems is a crucial frontier in modern science. It is a key focus of the science of complexity, an interdisciplinary field that seeks to understand systems with emergent properties and non-linear behaviors. This field is leading the development of non-equilibrium thermodynamics, which aims to provide a more comprehensive framework for analyzing open systems. However, a generalized theory that encompasses all types of open systems remains elusive.

The work of Ilya Prigogine, a Nobel laureate in thermodynamics, offers profound insights into the evolution of open systems. Prigogine's research explored how open systems, far from settling into a static equilibrium, can evolve in complex and unexpected ways. He suggested that these systems can approach a chaotic state due to the interplay of numerous factors. In this chaotic state, even infinitesimal disturbances within the system can lead to significant transformations, giving rise to what he termed "order out of chaos.

This phenomenon, also known as "self-organization through dissipative structures" or "bifurcation mode," highlights the remarkable ability of open systems to generate new structures and patterns of organization. Prigogine's work challenged the traditional thermodynamic view of systems inevitably progressing towards equilibrium. He demonstrated that open systems, fueled by the constant flow of energy and matter, can evolve towards greater complexity and organization.

However, applying Prigogine's theories to specific open systems can be challenging. The framework he developed is highly nuanced and varies depending on the system's unique characteristics. This complexity makes it difficult to formulate a simple, universal description of open systems.

Importantly, Prigogine's work shows that we cannot simply assume that open systems will inevitably reach a pessimistic equilibrium state, as is the case with isolated or closed systems. Instead, open systems have the potential for both positive and negative evolution. While a generalized theory remains elusive, countless examples from experience and scientific research suggest that individuals, groups, and living organisms are more likely to thrive and evolve positively when they embrace openness rather than isolation.

Beyond boundaries: Innovation through Openness

Chapter 1

The Beginning of
an Open System

A lifelong learning attitude is
directly connected to humility,
open-mindedness,
a willingness to take risks,
the ability to listen to others,
and the ability to honestly reflect on oneself.

- Harvard Professor John Kotter

Beyond boundaries: Innovation through Openness

Are you closed?
Or are you open?

The characteristics of a boundary can be natural or artificial.
Moreover, the characteristics of that boundary can change over time.
In nature, boundaries often occur naturally or exist in a fixed state.
Over time, the characteristics of those boundaries
may remain unchanged, or they may change.

Curiosity and challenge are the keys to opening closed boundaries

Curiosity and a willingness to challenge the status quo are essential for breaking through closed boundaries and exploring new frontiers. Consider the film Interstellar, released in 2014, which captivated audiences worldwide, including in Korea. The film depicts a future where Earth faces a devastating food crisis, forcing humanity to venture into the vast expanse of space in search of solutions.

The very title, Interstellar, meaning "between stars," suggests a narrative that transcends the confines of a closed world. It speaks to the boundless possibilities that emerge when we embrace an open perspective, connecting different worlds and exploring the unknown. The film's premise, with its focus on space exploration and the search for new habitable planets, embodies the spirit of curiosity and the courage to challenge existing limitations.

Just like in the film Interstellar, science has long grappled with the question of how systems evolve over time. Will they flourish and grow, or will they degenerate and ultimately disappear? To answer this question, natural science often employs a specific methodology: a system is defined within the vastness of the cosmos, and a boundary is drawn to separate it from its surroundings-everything else in the universe.

By carefully observing the exchanges and interactions that occur across this boundary, scientists can infer how the system will evolve. This approach allows us to examine how the system changes-whether it progresses or regresses-over time and under the influence of various factors.

The nature of the boundary plays a critical role in shaping the system's destiny. A rigid, impermeable boundary will isolate the system, limiting its interactions and potentially hindering its development. Conversely, a flexible, porous boundary allows for a greater exchange of energy and matter, fostering interactions that can drive the system's evolution and growth.

Understanding the characteristics of boundaries, therefore, is essential for comprehending the dynamics of systems and predicting their future trajectories.

A system can have a single boundary or multiple boundaries, each with its own unique characteristics. A boundary that allows for the unrestricted exchange of anything-information, matter, knowledge, tradition, culture, and so on-between the system and its surroundings is called an open boundary. Open boundaries facilitate the free flow of resources and ideas, fostering interaction and dynamic exchange.

On the other hand, a boundary that completely prevents any exchange between the system and its surroundings is called an isolated boundary. Isolated systems are self-contained and do not interact with their environment. A boundary that allows for the exchange of some things but not others is called a closed boundary. Closed systems can exchange energy with their surroundings, but not matter.

Returning to the story of Interstellar, humanity faces a critical choice as Earth becomes increasingly uninhabitable. Plan A involves developing a spaceship capable of carrying all of humanity to a new home. However, this ambitious plan requires groundbreaking technology to control gravity, a seemingly insurmountable challenge. Plan B, a more desperate measure, involves sending a select group with fertilized eggs to a new planet to ensure the survival of the human species.

Remarkably, in the film, humanity ultimately achieves the seemingly impossible Plan A through their pursuit of Plan B. This outcome highlights the power of embracing an open-system approach. By venturing beyond the confines of their dying planet and exploring the vastness of space, humanity unlocks new knowledge and possibilities, ultimately finding a solution that transcends their initial limitations.

The film Interstellar provides a powerful illustration of our understanding of systems and boundaries. When Earth faces a devastating food crisis and humanity loses its capacity for space travel, they become trapped within an isolated boundary, cut off from the possibilities of the wider universe.

However, with the launch of Plan B, a select group of humans ventures beyond Earth, carrying the hopes of humanity with them. While the majority remains on Earth, this bold step signifies a crucial shift—a transition from an isolated boundary to a closed one. By crossing the threshold and pursuing new possibilities, they break free from complete isolation.

Remarkably, during their journey for Plan B, humanity solves the seemingly insurmountable problem of gravity control. This breakthrough allows them to evacuate Earth and enter the open boundary of space, a realm of infinite possibilities. Interstellar powerfully demonstrates the transformative potential of embracing an open system.

Just as in the film, a single world or system, like Earth, must strive towards open boundaries to survive and thrive. This is not merely a product of cinematic imagination; it is supported by countless research findings and scientific evidence.

The characteristics of a boundary can be natural or artificial, and they can change over time. In the natural world, boundaries often arise organically and may appear fixed. However, natural events or human actions can alter these boundaries, leading to profound changes in the system's dynamics and evolutionary trajectory.

While natural science and engineering often deal with systems involving matter, energy, or entropy, the concept of a system extends far beyond these physical entities. When we consider individuals, groups, nations, or even human civilizations as systems, the boundaries that define them become more nuanced and often artificial. We have the power to consciously shape these boundaries, opening them to facilitate exchange, closing them for protection, or even isolating them entirely. This means that the evolution of these systems is heavily influenced by our intentions and choices[2].

To illustrate this concept, consider the evolution of photography. Most cameras today are digital, providing instant feedback on the image captured. However, in the era of analog cameras, we had to rely on intuition and patience. We couldn't see the results of our efforts until the film was developed, often days later. The excitement of finally seeing the photos was sometimes mixed with disappointment when mistakes or missed opportunities became apparent. This lack of immediate feedback highlights the challenges of navigating a system with limited information and control.

Similarly, in the realm of human systems, the boundaries we create-whether consciously or unconsciously-shape our interactions and influence our development. By understanding the nature of these boundaries and their impact on our lives, we can make more informed choices and strive towards a more open and interconnected world.

However, it wasn't the digital camera that first addressed this inconvenience, but the Polaroid camera. This ingenious invention

2. Ki-Pung Yoo, 「Energy and Thermodynamics」, Ajin Press, 2000.

allowed people to see their photos instantly by printing them on the spot using special coated paper.

The Polaroid camera was the brainchild of Edwin Land, a brilliant scholar of optics. The inspiration for this groundbreaking invention came from a simple question posed by his young daughter during a family vacation. Perplexed by the delay between taking a picture and seeing the result, she asked, "Why can't we see the picture right away?"

This innocent question sparked a creative fire in Land's mind. He envisioned a new type of photographic paper that combined the film and the print, allowing for instant development. This vision led to the birth of the Polaroid camera, a technology that revolutionized photography and brought instant gratification to countless picture-takers around the world.

The story of the Polaroid camera exemplifies the power of curiosity and the importance of questioning the status quo. It highlights how even seemingly simple questions can lead to profound innovations that change the way we interact with the world.

Traditional film captured images simultaneously with exposure to light, but it was extremely sensitive to external light. It had to be carefully shielded within a light-tight camera body and transported to a photo lab for development. Polaroid film, on the other hand, was revolutionary. It acted as both film and photographic paper, capturing the image and then emerging from the camera ready to be viewed. This seemingly simple alteration to the film's properties fundamentally changed the closed mechanism of traditional photography, opening up a world of instant gratification and convenience.

However, the true catalyst for this innovation was Edwin Land's open-mindedness. He didn't dismiss his young daughter's curiosity but instead embraced it as an opportunity for exploration and discovery. This receptiveness to new ideas, even those originating from a child, stands in stark contrast to the dismissive attitude often displayed by those who find children's inquisitiveness tiresome.

Creating an open world can sometimes happen by chance, through serendipitous encounters or unexpected questions. But it can also be a deliberate act, driven by a conscious desire for change and progress. Whether a system is open or closed, and how its boundaries are defined, can be a matter of autonomous choice or external pressure.

However, one thing remains certain: for a system to truly evolve and develop, it must embrace openness. An 'open system' with an 'open boundary' allows for the free flow of information, energy, and ideas, fostering innovation and growth. This is the central message I aim to convey in this book: the transformative power of openness.

Throughout history, the rise and fall of individuals, societies, and entire civilizations have been shaped by their openness or lack thereof. By examining these examples, I hope to illuminate the profound impact of open systems and inspire young people to embrace a mindset of openness and interconnectedness.

Young people, I implore you to tear down the walls that confine you. Open your minds to new ideas, new cultures, and new ways of thinking. Embrace diversity, challenge the status quo, and connect with the world around you. By opening your systems and your boundaries, you unlock the potential for boundless growth, innovation, and positive change.

The future belongs to those who dare to be open.

The first step of an open system, Prestigious universities are stepping outside the classroom

University professors must now act as guides and mentors, supporting students on their challenging journey of personal and intellectual growth. They must foster creativity and critical thinking, empowering students to become true leaders in a world that demands adaptability and innovation.

In today's era of rapid technological advancement and information explosion, knowledge is constantly evolving and expanding. Unlike the static information found in outdated textbooks, the world outside the classroom changes at an unprecedented pace. To stay relevant, both students and professors must cultivate an open mindset and actively engage with the world beyond their immediate boundaries. We must constantly seek new knowledge, challenge our assumptions, and adapt to the ever-shifting landscape of information.

This is a demanding and daunting task, but it is essential for navigating the complexities of the 21st century. Those who cling to outdated knowledge and resist new ideas will quickly find themselves falling behind. The future belongs to those who embrace lifelong learning and cultivate the skills and mindset needed to thrive in an open and interconnected world.

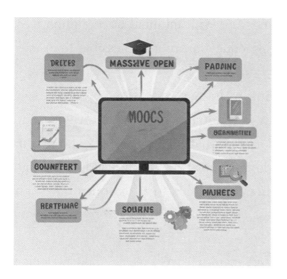

The rapid pace of change in the world is undeniable. The rise of big data, cloud computing, Wikipedia, and Massive Open Online Courses (MOOCs) are just a few examples of this transformation. MOOCs, in particular, represent a revolutionary idea. They allow anyone with an internet connection to access lectures from leading experts in various fields, regardless of their location or academic background.

Imagine a young person in Seoul with a strong command of English. Through MOOCs, they can attend lectures by renowned professors from top universities around the world, all without leaving their home. This accessibility is truly groundbreaking.

Recently, the concept of the online People's University, which originated in the western United States, has been gaining traction. This innovative approach systematically organizes MOOCs, providing a structured learning experience for those who want to acquire academic knowledge online. And with minimal or no tuition fees, these programs are making education more accessible than ever before.

This is a true revolution in higher education. By effectively utilizing these resources, individuals can gain knowledge and skills that rival, or even surpass, what traditional brick-and-mortar universities offer. The democratization of knowledge through technology is empowering individuals to take control of their learning journey and access opportunities that were previously out of reach.

Imagine a future where companies like Google or Apple no longer prioritize traditional academic credentials when hiring college graduates. Instead of focusing on the specific university attended, the major declared, or the GPA achieved, they prioritize candidates who have completed specialized online courses aligned with the company's specific needs. These courses might be offered through platforms like People's University or MOOCs, providing students with targeted, industry-relevant skills and knowledge.

This shift in hiring practices could trigger a massive upheaval in higher education. Traditional offline universities, especially those that fail to adapt to the changing demands of the job market, could face declining enrollment and financial struggles, potentially leading to closures.

Even in Korea, we could see a dramatic shift towards online learning. Imagine a single renowned professor delivering lectures to students across all universities nationwide through a centralized online platform. This scenario could lead to the closure of many second-tier universities that primarily focus on traditional classroom-based education.

This radical paradigm shift, once a concept confined to science fiction, could become our reality sooner than we think. The rise of online learning and the evolving needs of the job market are challenging the long-held assumptions about the value of a traditional university degree. The future of higher education may lie in a more flexible, personalized, and skills-focused approach, where individuals can curate their own learning journey and acquire the knowledge and competencies that are most relevant to their career aspirations.

In the traditional classroom, professors often adopt a didactic approach, lecturing as if they are the sole possessors of knowledge and expecting students to passively absorb information. This one-way, knowledge-dumping method is no longer effective in today's dynamic and interconnected world.

To cultivate creativity and critical thinking in young minds, we need a two-way, open educational revolution. The focus should shift from passive lectures to active discussions, where students are encouraged to question, analyze, and contribute their own perspectives. We need to empower students to become self-directed learners, capable of navigating the vast sea of information available to them.

In this age of instant access to information through smartphones and the internet, simply providing knowledge is no longer enough. Instead, educators must focus on igniting a passion for learning within students. We must teach them how to effectively search for, evaluate, and apply information, equipping them with the skills necessary to thrive in a world of constant change and innovation.

The IT revolution has ushered in an era of unprecedented global interconnectedness, with English emerging as the dominant language of the digital realm. Over 99% of information in the cyber and virtual world is in English, making it an essential tool for anyone who aspires to be part of the global intellectual community. While it's crucial to value and preserve one's native language, young people in non-English-speaking countries must recognize the importance of acquiring English proficiency. In this increasingly interconnected world, English has become as essential as the air we breathe or the water we drink. It serves as a bridge connecting individuals and cultures across the globe.

If older generations cling to outdated teaching methods and fail to adapt to this new reality, they risk becoming irrelevant in the education of young people who are growing up in an open, interconnected world. This disconnect could have far-reaching consequences.

In the 21st century, we are witnessing a major civilizational paradigm shift. As physical and mental boundaries between nations erode, a homogenizing force is at play. A select few elites, a single dominant language like English, a handful of advanced nations, a few prestigious international universities, and a limited number of top-tier products that meet global standards may rise to the forefront. Everything else risks being swept aside.

This trend towards globalization, while offering many opportunities, also carries the potential for cultural homogenization and the erosion of diversity. We must be mindful of these challenges and strive to preserve our unique cultural identities while embracing the interconnectedness of the modern world.

It's undeniable: we live in a world fraught with uncertainty and rapid change. The forces of globalization, technological disruption, and social upheaval are reshaping our reality at an unprecedented pace. In the face of these challenges, retreating into isolation is not an option. We cannot afford to cling to outdated paradigms and closed systems.

Now, more than ever, we must boldly open our boundaries. We must embrace new ideas, engage with different perspectives, and connect with the world around us. This openness is not merely a matter of choice; it is essential for our survival and growth.

By breaking down the walls that divide us, we can unlock the potential for innovation, collaboration, and collective progress. We can create a more inclusive, resilient, and dynamic world where everyone has the opportunity to thrive.

The time for hesitation is over. Let us embrace the challenge and step boldly into an open future.

Mpemba effect, breaking down prejudices is the beginning of an open system

There's a fascinating scientific phenomenon known as the Mpemba effect, named after Erasto Mpemba, a Tanzanian student who made a surprising discovery in the 1960s. During a high school cooking class, Mpemba and his classmates were making ice cream. The recipe required boiling the mixture to properly combine the ingredients.

To cool his hot mixture quickly, Mpemba decided to place it directly into the freezer, contrary to the instructions. He expected it to take longer to freeze than his classmates' mixtures, which had been cooled to room temperature beforehand. However, to his surprise, Mpemba's hot mixture froze faster.

When Mpemba shared his observation with his teacher and classmates, they dismissed it as impossible. However, Mpemba persisted. When a physics professor from a nearby university visited the school, Mpemba seized the opportunity to share his discovery. Intrigued, the professor conducted experiments and confirmed the phenomenon, which later became known as the Mpemba effect.

This story highlights how preconceived notions and established knowledge can sometimes hinder scientific progress. People often resist new ideas that challenge their understanding of the world. In the case of the Mpemba effect, the prevailing belief that hotter water should take longer to freeze prevented many from accepting Mpemba's observation.

The Mpemba effect serves as a powerful reminder to remain open to new possibilities, even those that seem to defy conventional wisdom. If we had been Mpemba's friends or teacher, would we have had the open-mindedness to accept his observation and explore its implications? Or would we have dismissed it as an anomaly, blinded by our preconceptions?

Solar power, which harnesses sunlight to generate electricity, offers a clean and sustainable alternative to fossil fuels. It produces no harmful emissions and relies on a virtually inexhaustible resource: the sun. However, despite its environmental benefits, the widespread adoption of solar power is often hindered by economic considerations.

The utilization of any technology, even one with clear environmental advantages, is often determined by its economic viability. Solar power is a prime example. As long as fossil fuels remain the dominant and most cost-effective energy source, alternative technologies like solar power struggle to compete.

However, this dynamic can shift when the price of fossil fuels rises. As fossil fuels become more expensive, previously developed renewable energy technologies become increasingly attractive. Solar power, in particular, gains attention during such periods of market fluctuation.

The reason for this lies in the cost-benefit ratio. Currently, the amount of energy generated by solar power relative to the initial investment in equipment is relatively low compared to fossil fuels.

However, if fossil fuel prices rise significantly, the cost of investing in solar power becomes comparatively more affordable.

Ultimately, even the cleanest technologies cannot escape the scrutiny of economic evaluation. Market forces and cost-effectiveness play a crucial role in determining which energy sources are adopted and utilized on a large scale. The transition to a more sustainable energy future will likely depend on a combination of technological advancements, environmental awareness, and favorable economic conditions.

The limitations of solar power on Earth are largely due to the specific conditions of our planet. Earth's atmosphere, while essential for life, acts as a filter, reducing the amount of sunlight that reaches the surface. From the perspective of solar power generation, this is a significant drawback.

However, by venturing beyond Earth's atmosphere, we can unlock the full potential of solar energy. Space Solar Power (SSP), a concept that has been explored for decades, offers a tantalizing solution. Imagine a network of satellites in Earth's orbit, continuously collecting solar energy and beaming it back to Earth. These satellites would be free from the limitations of atmospheric interference and day-night cycles, providing a constant and abundant source of clean energy.

While SSP is still in the research and development phase, it represents a fascinating example of how expanding our boundaries can lead to groundbreaking innovations. By stepping outside the confines of Earth's closed system, we can access a virtually limitless supply of solar energy and potentially revolutionize the way we power our world.

The pursuit of SSP embodies the spirit of open systems. It encourages us to challenge our assumptions, explore new frontiers, and seek solutions beyond the limitations of our current environment. Just as the film Interstellar depicted humanity venturing into space to overcome the challenges on Earth, SSP represents a bold step towards a more sustainable and abundant energy future.

The first law of thermodynamics states that energy cannot be created or destroyed, only transformed from one form to another. However, while the total amount of energy in the universe remains constant, the amount of usable energy decreases over time. This is due to the second law of thermodynamics, which states that entropy, or disorder, tends to increase in closed systems.

We humans consume energy voraciously in our pursuit of comfort and convenience. We rely heavily on fossil fuels like coal and petroleum, which, while providing energy, also contribute to environmental degradation and climate change. As we deplete these finite resources, we are not only reducing the amount of usable energy available but also pushing our planet towards an irreversible state of environmental decline.

Within the closed system of Earth, we are bound to face limitations. Our resources are finite, and our actions have consequences that ripple throughout the interconnected web of life. Consider the example of beef consumption. To satisfy the demand for beef, vast herds of cattle are raised, requiring extensive land and resources. This demand has fueled deforestation, particularly in the Amazon rainforest, a vital ecosystem that plays a crucial role in regulating the global climate.

Many societies, particularly in the West, have become accustomed to meat-centric diets. However, persisting in these unsustainable patterns will inevitably lead to a closed system, where resources are depleted, and environmental damage becomes irreversible. We must actively strive to break free from these unsustainable practices and embrace a more balanced and sustainable approach to consumption.

Recognizing the limitations of our current systems and making conscious choices to reduce our environmental impact is crucial for ensuring a healthy and thriving planet for future generations.

In his influential book Entropy: A New World View, Jeremy Rifkin argues that human actions, particularly those aimed at manipulating nature for comfort and convenience, inevitably lead to an increase in entropy. He criticizes the disproportionate energy consumption of industrialized nations, pointing out that less than 6% of the world's population consumes a third of the world's energy.

Rifkin extends his critique to the development of alternative energy sources like solar power and recycling. He argues that even these seemingly environmentally friendly practices contribute to entropy increase within the closed system of Earth. While these technologies offer some benefits, they still require energy and resources for their production and implementation, ultimately generating waste and contributing to the overall degradation of the planet.

Rifkin advocates for a fundamental shift in our approach to energy consumption. He argues that the burden of reducing energy use should not fall disproportionately on those who already consume less. Instead, he proposes a progressive approach, where those who consume more energy bear a greater responsibility for reducing their consumption. Just as those with higher incomes pay more taxes, those who use more energy should be encouraged to adopt more sustainable practices.

This requires a change in the mindset and habits of those accustomed to the comforts of mass consumption. We must challenge the prevailing notion that endless economic growth and material consumption are sustainable or even desirable. Without addressing the root causes of excessive energy use and shifting towards a more mindful and responsible approach to consumption, we cannot hope to create a truly sustainable future.

Breaking free from the limitations of a closed system requires a fundamental shift in our values and behaviors. We must recognize that our planet's resources are finite and that our actions have far-reaching consequences. Only by embracing a more sustainable and equitable approach to energy consumption can we hope to move towards a boundless future where both humanity and the planet can thrive.

The journey towards an open system begins with a willingness to challenge ingrained prejudices and question conventional wisdom. Often, our deeply held beliefs and assumptions, even those we consider "common sense," can blind us to new possibilities and hinder our understanding of the world.

Prejudice begets prejudice, creating a cycle of narrow-mindedness that limits our potential for growth and innovation. To truly embrace an open system, we must be willing to overturn these prejudices, especially those related to science and the natural world.

By questioning our assumptions and seeking new perspectives, we can break free from the constraints of limited thinking and open ourselves to a world of possibilities. This willingness to challenge the status quo is essential for fostering creativity, driving progress, and creating a more open and inclusive society.

Yes, let's sometimes look at Ourselves on Earth from outside the Earth

The Tang Dynasty poet Bai Juyi(白居易), in his poem 'To Wine(對酒),' writes, 'What are they fighting for on a snail's horn? Life is as fleeting as lightning.' This poignant verse reminds us of the futility of petty conflicts and the ephemeral nature of our existence. We humans, inhabiting this tiny planet Earth, a mere speck in a vast cosmic ocean of 100 billion galaxies, often lose sight of the bigger picture.

To cultivate an open mind, we must expand our horizons and embrace a broader perspective. A wider perspective fosters broader thinking, allowing us to transcend the limitations of our immediate surroundings. If our focus remains solely on Earth, we cannot grasp the immensity of the universe that lies beyond.

Ensnared in the relentless pursuit of success and material gain, we rarely pause to contemplate the vastness of the cosmos. We chase after time, fixated on those ahead of us in the competitive race of life. But can we break free from this self-imposed confinement of time and space?

Even if our physical bodies are bound to Earth, our minds can soar among the stars. Let us contemplate the boundless expanse of the universe, a realm that dwarfs our individual and collective systems. Even modern science, with all its advancements, cannot definitively measure the universe's true size. Its vastness remains shrouded in speculation and inference, limited by the boundaries of human imagination and the challenges of empirical observation.

By acknowledging the limitations of our current understanding and embracing the vast unknown, we open ourselves to new possibilities and cultivate a sense of wonder and humility. This shift in perspective can liberate us from the confines of our limited worldview and inspire us to embrace a more open and interconnected existence.

How should we perceive the universe as a system? Is it an infinitely open and boundless expanse, or is it a closed and isolated entity with finite limits? Let's postpone this debate for now and attempt to grasp the sheer scale of the cosmos.

Imagine, for a moment, that the universe is infinitely large. In this boundless expanse, our entire galaxy, with its hundreds of billions of stars, is but a tiny grain of sand. Within this grain of sand, our solar system is a mere speck of dust, and Earth, our home planet, is an even smaller speck within that. And on this minuscule Earth, we humans inhabit a tiny corner, living our lives in a fleeting moment of time.

From this perspective, a human life seems utterly insignificant, a transient flicker in the grand tapestry of the cosmos. Yet, we often become consumed by the anxieties and struggles of our daily existence, losing sight of the vastness that surrounds us.

A thousand years ago, the poet Bai Juyi, contemplating the brevity of life while sipping a cup of wine, captured this sentiment in his timeless verse. He understood that our earthly concerns, when viewed against the backdrop of the universe's immensity, often appear trivial and fleeting.

Even modern science, with all its advancements, struggles to comprehend the full extent of the universe. Its true size remains a mystery, shrouded in speculation and inference. The limitations of human imagination and the challenges of empirical observation make it difficult to grasp the sheer scale of the cosmos.

By acknowledging the vastness of the universe and our relatively small place within it, we can gain a sense of perspective and humility. This expanded worldview can liberate us from the confines of our limited perspectives and inspire us to embrace a more open and interconnected existence.

Let's contemplate the temporal dimension of our existence. Does time, as we perceive it, truly exist? When and how did this universe, with its intricate dance of galaxies and stars, come into being? From what primordial state did it emerge, and how has it evolved over billions of years into the cosmos we observe today? How long has the universe existed, and how far into the future can our imaginations stretch?

These questions, fundamental to our understanding of existence, remain shrouded in mystery. No one can definitively answer them. In this vast expanse of space and the seemingly endless continuum of time, we grapple with the challenge of defining our place, our civilizations, and our individual lives.

When we gaze at the stars twinkling in the night sky, we are peering into the past. The light that reaches our eyes has journeyed across unimaginable distances, carrying with it the echoes of events that occurred hundreds, thousands, or even millions of years ago. It's a truly awe-inspiring realization. Perhaps it is in moments like these, when we confront the vastness of time and space, that our minds begin to expand beyond the confines of our everyday experiences.

There's a saying, "a bird's-eye view." When we are immersed in the details of our lives, focused on the immediate surroundings, we often fail to grasp the bigger picture. But when we ascend to a higher vantage point, a new perspective unfolds. We see the interconnectedness of things, the patterns and relationships that were previously hidden from view.

Similarly, when we contemplate the vastness of the universe and the long sweep of cosmic time, we gain a new appreciation for our place within this grand scheme. We recognize the limitations of our individual perspectives and the importance of cultivating a broader, more encompassing view of reality.

By shifting our perspective, by expanding our awareness beyond the confines of our immediate concerns, we open ourselves to new possibilities and deeper understanding. We discover new truths, new connections, and new ways of being. This is the essence of an open system—a willingness to embrace the unknown, to challenge our assumptions, and to explore the boundless possibilities that lie beyond our current horizons.

You feel stagnant?
That's what happens when you're
in a closed energetic system

Let's consider a living human being as a complex and dynamic open system. If we define the individual as the system and the rest of the world as its surroundings, we can observe a constant flow of exchange across the open boundary that separates them.

To sustain life, a human being must take in essential resources like food, water, and oxygen from the surroundings. These resources provide the energy and building blocks necessary for growth, maintenance, and repair. At the same time, the human body expels waste products such as carbon dioxide, urine, and feces, returning them to the environment.

Beyond these basic physiological needs, humans also interact with their surroundings in more complex ways. We create and utilize tools, build shelters, and develop technologies to enhance our comfort and well-being. These actions involve the exchange of materials and energy across the boundary between the individual and the environment.

Furthermore, to cultivate our humanity and contribute to society, we engage in a constant exchange of information and knowledge. Through education, we acquire knowledge and skills from others. We internalize this information, process it, and then share it with others through communication and collaboration.

This continuous exchange of matter, energy, and information is essential for human flourishing. Just as an open system thrives on interaction with its surroundings, so too do humans depend on a dynamic and reciprocal relationship with the world around them. By embracing openness and engaging in meaningful exchange with our environment and with each other, we can foster growth, innovation, and collective progress.

We humans are constantly interacting with the world around us, exchanging thoughts, emotions, and experiences through the permeable boundaries that define our individual selves. But what would happen if these boundaries were to become impermeable, preventing any exchange with the outside world?

Imagine a human being completely isolated from their surroundings, unable to take in sustenance, expel waste, or engage in any form of communication or interaction. In this scenario, the human system, deprived of the vital flow of energy and information, would gradually decline and ultimately cease to function. This inevitable outcome is analogous to the concept of equilibrium in thermodynamics.

In thermodynamics, equilibrium describes a state where a system, isolated from its surroundings, reaches a point of maximum entropy. All internal gradients and differences disappear, and the system becomes uniform and unchanging. For a living organism, this state of equilibrium represents death. Life thrives on exchange and interaction; without it, the delicate balance that sustains life collapses.

This analogy highlights the crucial importance of openness

for human well-being and development. Just as a living organism requires a constant flow of energy and matter to survive, so too do we humans need social interaction, intellectual stimulation, and emotional connection to thrive. Isolation, whether physical or emotional, can lead to stagnation, decline, and ultimately, the cessation of our vital functions.

By embracing openness, by engaging in meaningful exchange with the world around us, we nourish our minds, bodies, and spirits. We foster growth, creativity, and resilience. We become active participants in the dynamic dance of life, contributing to the rich tapestry of human experience.

The characteristics of a system can profoundly influence the trajectory of a human life, shaping everything from our personality and social interactions to our overall well-being. Consider a typical individual who actively engages with the world around them, freely exchanging ideas, resources, and experiences. It's often observed that such open-minded individuals tend to be more sociable and thrive in collaborative environments. Conversely, those who isolate themselves and resist interaction with their surroundings may struggle to form meaningful connections and experience a diminished sense of belonging.

Research suggests that individuals who choose the tragic path of suicide often exhibit traits of extreme introversion and social isolation. Their closed-off nature may prevent them from seeking help or forming the supportive relationships that can buffer against despair. On the other hand, individuals who achieve positions of influence and leadership often possess open personalities, readily engaging with others and embracing new ideas and experiences.

This correlation between openness and success can be understood through the lens of system dynamics. Open systems, characterized by the free exchange of energy and information, are inherently more adaptable and resilient. They can readily respond to changes in their environment and evolve in ways that closed systems cannot.

Interestingly, the concept of openness even finds parallels in the evolution of the universe itself. Modern physics suggests that in the early universe, matter and antimatter existed in equal amounts. However, during a period of intense instability and self-organization, a phenomenon known as symmetry breaking occurred. Antimatter vanished, leaving matter to dominate the universe as we know it.

This symmetry breaking event, a pivotal moment in the universe's history, highlights the potential for unexpected and transformative change that can arise from a state of openness and instability. Just as the universe evolved through a process of dynamic interaction and exchange, so too can human beings thrive by embracing openness and engaging with the world around them.

While modern physics explores the concept of symmetry breaking and the dominance of matter over antimatter, a similar concept has existed in Eastern thought for centuries. In traditional Eastern medicine, the concept of "ki" (氣) plays a central role. "Ki" is often translated as "vital energy" or "life force," and it is believed to flow through the body, animating and sustaining life.

When faced with challenges or setbacks, people often say, "My 'ki' is blocked." This expression reflects the belief that disruptions in the flow of "ki" can lead to physical and emotional imbalances. While it may seem like a leap to connect this ancient concept to modern physics, there are intriguing parallels.

Just as the universe maintains a delicate balance between matter and antimatter, Eastern medicine emphasizes the importance of maintaining a harmonious flow of "ki" alongside the circulation of blood. Blood, the physical carrier of oxygen and nutrients, flows through a complex network of blood vessels. Similarly, "ki" is believed to circulate through invisible channels, known as meridians, connecting the various organs and systems of the body.

Eastern medicine posits that blockages in the flow of "ki" can lead to illness and disease, just as blockages in blood vessels can disrupt circulation and cause harm. Therefore, practices like acupuncture and moxibustion aim to stimulate the flow of "ki" and restore balance within the body.

This emphasis on the circulation of "ki" resonates with the concept of open systems. Just as an open system thrives on the free exchange of energy and information, so too does the human body depend on the unimpeded flow of "ki" for optimal health and vitality. Each subsystem within the body must be open and interconnected to maintain the dynamic equilibrium that sustains life.

By exploring the parallels between modern physics, Eastern medicine, and the concept of open systems, we can gain a deeper appreciation for the interconnectedness of all things and the importance of maintaining balance and flow in our lives.

In a poignant scene from a Japanese film, a character facing their final moments reflects on the nature of existence: 'With cold hands and a frozen heart, on the verge of departing this world, to truly see humanity and all things is perhaps to achieve a profound understanding—a harmonious blend of analytical observation and intuitive insight.'

This insightful reflection speaks to the duality of human experience, the interplay between our rational minds and our intuitive hearts. It suggests that true understanding arises from a synthesis of these two modes of knowing, a harmonious balance between the analytical and the artistic.

The character continues, 'This understanding might also be akin to the act of persistently moving forward, in other words, 'will'.' This observation highlights the inherent drive within us to explore, to learn, and to evolve. It's a testament to the enduring human spirit, the unwavering will that propels us forward even in the face of adversity.

'It's a mystery that humans can comprehend the world,' the character muses, 'but it's an even greater mystery that something born from nothing can possess will.' This profound statement captures the awe and wonder that arise when we contemplate the origins of consciousness and the driving force behind our existence.

Life is indeed a tapestry woven with countless mysteries. Yet, amidst these enigmas, there exists an underlying flow, an interconnectedness that binds all things together. To understand this flow, to perceive the intricate relationships and dynamic exchanges that shape our reality, is to grasp the essence of an open system.

By delving into the mysteries of the universe's creation, by exploring the fundamental forces that govern the cosmos, we can begin to perceive this open system in its full grandeur. We can witness the intricate dance of energy and matter, the ceaseless flow of creation and destruction, and the interconnectedness that binds all things together.

Learning is
a reverse evolutionary process

Let's delve into the concept of open and closed systems using a relatable example: a classroom bustling with students. Picture a scenario where dozens of students are crammed into a small, stuffy classroom. To simplify our analysis, let's assume this classroom has an isolated boundary. This means no heat, air, or any other substance can be exchanged with the outside environment. We'll also assume there's enough air inside for everyone to breathe comfortably for the duration of the 75-minute class.

In this scenario, the classroom can be considered an isolated system, although in reality, it's probably closer to a closed system. Why? Because even with the doors and windows shut, there might still be some minor air leakage or heat transfer through the walls. However, for the sake of our illustration, we'll treat it as an isolated system where no exchange occurs.

Initially, the air within the classroom is a relatively homogenous mix, composed mainly of oxygen and nitrogen, with a small amount of carbon dioxide exhaled by the students and the professor. However, this peaceful equilibrium is suddenly disrupted when the professor, perhaps lost in the depths of their lecture, experiences a natural bodily function—a fart.

This unexpected emission introduces new elements into the

classroom's atmosphere. Farts are primarily composed of nitrogen, hydrogen, carbon dioxide, and methane, along with trace amounts of other volatile compounds that contribute to their distinctive aroma. These gases, initially concentrated in the professor's immediate vicinity, begin to diffuse throughout the classroom, altering the composition of the air and potentially causing a ripple of reactions among the students.

While this event might elicit a few giggles or wrinkled noses, it serves as an excellent illustration of how even seemingly small changes can disrupt the equilibrium of a closed system. The introduction of new elements, even in gaseous form, alters the overall composition of the system and can trigger a cascade of effects.

Let's rewind to the moment the professor, standing at the podium, releases that unexpected burst of flatulence. The gaseous components of the fart, initially concentrated around the podium, don't just linger in the air. Instead, they embark on a journey of spontaneous dispersion, spreading throughout the classroom.

This phenomenon, known as diffusion in physical science, is a natural process that occurs whenever there's a difference in concentration between two areas. Substances, whether they're gases, liquids, or even solids, naturally move from regions of high concentration to regions of low concentration. Think of it like a crowded room gradually emptying as people spread out to find more space.

The speed of this diffusion is directly proportional to the concentration difference. The greater the difference, the faster the substance spreads. In our classroom scenario, the fart gases quickly disperse from their initial high concentration near the professor to the lower concentration areas throughout the room. This is why, much to the students' amusement or dismay, the evidence of the professor's indiscretion soon becomes universally apparent.

This humorous example illustrates a fundamental principle of nature: systems tend to move towards a state of equilibrium. In this case, the fart gases diffuse until they are evenly distributed throughout the classroom, eliminating the concentration difference. This natural tendency towards equilibrium is a driving force behind many physical and chemical processes.

Even if the professor tries to maintain a facade of innocence, the students, with their newly acquired olfactory evidence, will likely exchange knowing glances and stifled giggles. Meanwhile, the fart gases, oblivious to the social drama unfolding, continue their relentless journey of diffusion. They spread throughout the classroom until their concentration becomes uniform, reaching a state of equilibrium.

In this equilibrium state, the fart molecules are evenly distributed throughout the classroom, and there's no longer a concentration gradient to drive further diffusion. The system has reached a point of maximum entropy, where disorder is maximized, and no further spontaneous change will occur. It's as if the classroom air has collectively "forgotten" the initial burst of flatulence that triggered this whole process.

To return to the pre-fart state, where the fart gases were concentrated around the professor, would require an external intervention, like some kind of elaborate air purification system. This illustrates another important principle: reversing a spontaneous process, like diffusion, requires an input of energy.

This seemingly trivial example of a fart diffusing in a classroom encapsulates some profound truths about the nature of systems and their evolution. It highlights the tendency towards equilibrium, the irreversibility of spontaneous processes, and the cost of reversing those processes.

Furthermore, it hints at a somewhat pessimistic view of natural evolution. Just as the fart gases inevitably spread and homogenize, so too do many natural processes tend towards a state of increased disorder and uniformity. This raises questions about the long-term fate of the universe and the inevitable march towards equilibrium, a state often associated with stagnation and decay. However, as we'll explore later, open systems offer a glimmer of hope, demonstrating the potential for complexity, growth, and even the emergence of order from chaos.

Let's examine the process of learning through lectures in university life from the perspective of natural phenomena. How does this process align with, or deviate from, the natural tendencies of the universe?

If we consider a student as a system and the classroom as their environment, with an isolated or closed boundary between them, we encounter an interesting paradox. The direction of academic evolution, where students actively engage in learning and intellectual growth, seems to contradict the natural direction of evolution as described by thermodynamics.

In the natural world, systems tend towards equilibrium, a state of maximum entropy or disorder. Heat flows from hot to cold, substances diffuse from high concentration to low concentration, and living organisms age and eventually die. These processes occur spontaneously, driven by the inherent tendency towards increased entropy.

From this perspective, the effort required for students to focus on their studies, especially when faced with more enticing options like socializing or relaxing, seems to defy the natural order. When we are young, our instincts often urge us to play, to seek pleasure, and to avoid exertion. This inclination aligns with the natural tendency towards entropy, where systems gravitate towards states of lower energy and greater disorder.

Therefore, the pursuit of knowledge and intellectual growth appears to be a uniquely human endeavor, a conscious act of resistance against the natural flow of entropy. It requires effort, discipline, and a willingness to embrace challenges and discomfort. While playing and resting may align with the natural direction of human evolution, learning and growing require us to actively push against this tendency, to expend energy and create order from chaos.

While the natural world tends towards equilibrium, a state of maximum entropy and minimal energy, the trajectory of human evolution follows a different path. We humans strive to grow, to learn, and to achieve our full potential, a journey that often requires us to resist the pull of entropy and actively expend energy to create order and complexity.

It's crucial to remember that once a system reaches equilibrium, it cannot spontaneously return to its previous state. Reversing this process requires a significant investment of energy and effort. This principle applies to human development as well. If we succumb to inertia and allow our skills and knowledge to atrophy, regaining them later can be an arduous, if not impossible, task.

There's a time for everything, including diligent study and focused effort. The ancient proverb, "少年以老 學難成" ("It is easy for a young person to become old, but difficult to achieve learning"), encapsulates this wisdom. It reminds us that the time for learning and growth is often when we are young and possess the energy and adaptability to acquire new skills and knowledge.

The journey of youth is often characterized by a struggle against the natural inclination towards ease and comfort. Young people must resist the allure of distractions, the temptation to prioritize play over study, and the desire to succumb to inertia. They must actively engage in the pursuit of knowledge, even when it requires discipline, sacrifice, and a willingness to embrace discomfort.

By striving for growth and self-improvement, young people defy the natural tendency towards equilibrium. They slow down the inevitable march towards entropy, creating a unique and meaningful trajectory for their lives. This is the essence of human evolution—a conscious and deliberate effort to transcend our natural limitations and achieve our full potential.

When a cohort of students embarks on their university journey, they arrive with diverse backgrounds, motivations, and levels of preparedness. Some may possess a strong foundation of knowledge and a burning desire to learn, while others may be less academically inclined or motivated. This diversity is a natural part of any student population.

However, if these students are placed in an environment that lacks rigor and challenge, where academic excellence is not actively encouraged and rewarded, a detrimental phenomenon can occur. Instead of striving for intellectual growth and pushing against the natural tendency towards entropy, the students may succumb to inertia and complacency. This can lead to a "natural evolution" scenario, where the overall academic ability of the group regresses towards a lower common denominator.

Imagine a classroom where students receive good grades regardless of their effort or engagement. In such an environment, there is little incentive to strive for excellence. Students may become complacent, choosing comfort and ease over the challenges of intellectual exploration. This downward leveling effect can ultimately undermine the very purpose of higher education, which is to foster intellectual growth, critical thinking, and the pursuit of knowledge.

If universities fail to provide a stimulating and challenging environment that encourages students to reach their full potential, they risk becoming mere diploma mills, churning out graduates who lack the skills and knowledge necessary to thrive in a complex and demanding world. A true education requires effort, discipline, and a willingness to embrace challenges. It is a journey of transformation that pushes us beyond our comfort zones and helps us to achieve a higher level of understanding and capability.

To counter the natural tendency towards complacency and intellectual stagnation, professors must adopt a proactive approach that challenges students and encourages them to strive for excellence. This may involve implementing rigorous attendance policies, assigning frequent homework and exams, and fostering active participation through discussions and projects.

While these measures may initially be perceived as demanding or even unpleasant, they serve a crucial purpose. By creating an environment that encourages effort and engagement, professors can help students resist the pull of inertia and embrace the challenges of intellectual growth.

This approach can be likened to intentionally keeping students in a state of "productive discomfort." By pushing them beyond their comfort zones, professors can stimulate their curiosity, foster critical thinking, and cultivate a deeper understanding of the subject matter.

During my time as a teaching assistant, I often reminded students that even with natural talent, consistent effort and dedication are essential for achieving mastery. I challenged them with demanding assignments, rigorous exams, and complex projects, pushing them to reach their full potential. While some students may have initially resented this approach, many later expressed gratitude for the valuable skills and work ethic they developed.

The learning process can indeed be a challenging and even uncomfortable experience. It requires us to confront our limitations, embrace new ideas, and persevere through setbacks. However, it is through this process of struggle and growth that we truly develop our intellectual capacity and achieve a deeper understanding of ourselves and the world around us.

By embracing the challenges of learning, we defy the natural tendency towards entropy and embark on a journey of personal and intellectual transformation. This is the essence of education—a process of continuous growth and self-discovery that empowers us to reach our full potential and make meaningful contributions to the world.

To become a prestigious university, it must break down its closed boundaries

For the past few decades, South Korean universities have remained stagnant, clinging to outdated models and resisting change. This inward focus and resistance to innovation have left them ill-prepared for the rapid transformations occurring in the global landscape of higher education. Today, they stand precariously on the brink of a precipice, facing an uncertain future.

The question is, will our universities succumb to the forces of inertia and tumble over the edge, or will they seize this moment to critically examine their shortcomings and embrace a new era of openness and innovation?

The answer, I believe, lies in embracing the principles of an open system. Universities must break free from their insular mindset and actively engage with the world around them. They must foster collaboration, encourage interdisciplinary thinking, and embrace new technologies and pedagogical approaches.

By opening their doors to diverse perspectives, fostering a culture of experimentation and innovation, and actively engaging with the global community, South Korean universities can transform themselves into dynamic hubs of learning and creativity. They can become catalysts for progress, equipping students with the skills and knowledge necessary to thrive in an increasingly interconnected and rapidly changing world.

The choice is clear: embrace openness and adapt, or risk becoming relics of a bygone era. The future of South Korean universities hangs in the balance.

To not merely survive, but thrive in the face of intense domestic and international competition, universities must radically rethink their boundaries and embrace a new era of openness. They must dismantle the physical and metaphorical walls that confine them and actively engage in a dynamic exchange with the world around them.

Imagine a university where the free flow of people, ideas, and resources is not only encouraged but celebrated. A university where talented freshmen are welcomed, and outstanding faculty are recruited from around the globe. A university where research projects are pursued with vigor, and the latest global educational information is readily accessible. A university where resources, materials, and cutting-edge equipment are readily available to support learning and innovation.

This open university would be a vibrant hub of activity, with a constant influx of visiting scholars, researchers, and students from diverse backgrounds. It would also be a place where students are encouraged to complete their studies efficiently and move on to contribute their knowledge and skills to the wider world. Research findings, academic publications, and innovative ideas would flow outward, enriching the global intellectual community.

Professors would not be confined to their ivory towers but would actively engage in academic exchange and collaboration with colleagues around the world. They would attend conferences, conduct research abroad, and bring back valuable insights and knowledge to their home institution.

Of course, this open system would also require mechanisms for accountability and continuous improvement. Faculty who neglects their teaching or research responsibilities, and students who fail to engage in their studies, would face appropriate consequences. The university must maintain a dynamic environment where excellence is rewarded, and complacency is challenged.

By fostering a culture of openness, collaboration, and continuous learning, universities can become powerful engines of innovation and progress. They can equip students with the skills and knowledge necessary to navigate the complexities of the 21st century and contribute to a more just and sustainable world.

Achieving prestige in higher education is not an insurmountable task. While many factors contribute to a university's reputation, a key ingredient often overlooked is the commitment to fostering an open and dynamic learning environment.

The leadership of the university, including the board of directors, the president, and the tenured professors, must embrace an open mindset, welcoming new ideas, encouraging innovation, and actively engaging with the wider world. This openness sets the tone for the entire institution and creates a culture that values intellectual curiosity, critical thinking, and a willingness to challenge the status quo.

Furthermore, maintaining a certain level of tension and disequilibrium within the university is essential for driving continuous improvement and preventing stagnation. This can be achieved by setting high academic standards, providing challenging coursework, and fostering a competitive yet supportive learning environment.

By embracing openness and fostering a culture of intellectual rigor, universities can create a fertile ground for innovation, creativity, and academic excellence. This, in turn, will attract talented students and faculty, leading to a virtuous cycle of growth and prestige. The key to success lies not in resting on past laurels, but in constantly pushing the boundaries of knowledge and challenging oneself to reach new heights.

When we examine national university policies, it becomes evident that South Korea struggles with inefficiency in leveraging higher education to drive national development. Universities operate under a heavily regulated system, with significant government intervention in areas such as student selection, enrollment quotas, departmental structure, tuition fees, and overall administration. This restrictive environment stifles innovation, limits autonomy, and hinders universities from responding effectively to the evolving needs of the global knowledge economy.

In contrast, consider the example of Princeton University, a leading institution in the United States. Princeton enjoys a remarkable degree of autonomy, free from government interference in virtually all aspects of its operations. It sets its own admission standards, determines its curriculum, manages its finances, and governs itself according to market-driven principles.

This autonomy allows Princeton to attract top students and

faculty from around the world, cultivate a culture of academic excellence, and adapt quickly to the changing demands of the global landscape. It's no coincidence that the United States boasts the highest educational competitiveness globally, generating substantial revenue from international students who seek a world-class education and contribute to the country's talent pool.

Observing the stark contrast between the American and South Korean models, one cannot help but feel frustrated and concerned about the future of our universities. The current system, with its emphasis on control and regulation, hinders innovation and limits the potential of our institutions to compete on a global stage.

To enhance the competitiveness of South Korean universities, we must embrace a more autonomous and market-driven approach. By granting universities greater freedom to manage their affairs, set their own strategic priorities, and respond to the demands of the global knowledge economy, we can unlock their potential to become true engines of innovation and progress.

Compared to the more laissez-faire approach of the United States, South Korea's Ministry of Education has maintained a rigid and outdated regulatory framework for universities. From freshman recruitment and tuition policies to enrollment adjustments and curriculum design, nearly every aspect of university operations is subject to strict government oversight. This stifling control has created a closed system in higher education, hindering innovation and impeding progress.

As South Korea ascends to the ranks of advanced economies, our companies are increasingly competing on a global stage. However, the talent pool nurtured by our universities is falling short of the expectations and demands of these globally competitive firms. This mismatch is a direct consequence of the limitations imposed by excessive government control and regulation.

The need for reform in South Korea's university policies is long overdue. For over two decades, the system has remained largely unchanged, despite the rapid transformations occurring in the global knowledge economy. Now, the system teeters on the brink of collapse, struggling to keep pace with the demands of the 21st century.

South Korea's higher education system is in dire need of a change, and the government must take decisive action to grant universities, especially private ones, greater autonomy. This autonomy should cover various areas, allowing universities to set their own admission standards and select students based on merit, design innovative curricula that meet evolving needs, set their own tuition fees to generate resources for investment in faculty, facilities, and research, and manage their internal affairs, including staffing, resource allocation, and strategic direction.

By embracing a more autonomous and market-driven approach, South Korea's universities can unleash their potential to become dynamic centers of learning, innovation, and research. They can cultivate the talent needed to drive economic growth, foster social progress, and contribute to the nation's competitiveness on the global stage. The time for bold and decisive action is now.

Identifying the Root Causes of Stagnation. While the need for educational reform in South Korea is widely acknowledged, progress has been frustratingly slow. To overcome this inertia, we must identify the root causes of resistance and develop effective countermeasures. Who, or what, is hindering the flow of progress and preventing our universities from reaching their full potential?

Is it the head of state, the education minister, or high-ranking officials within the Ministry of Education? Are they clinging to outdated paradigms and resisting change due to bureaucratic inertia or vested interests? Or is the problem more systemic, embedded within the culture of the civil service and its emphasis on conformity and adherence to established procedures?

Perhaps the blame lies with the powerful influence of high-ranking civil servants who have successfully navigated the rigorous national examination system. These individuals, often products of a highly competitive and standardized education system, may be resistant to change and reluctant to embrace new ideas that challenge the status quo.

Another potential obstacle is the lack of genuine dialogue and collaboration between policymakers, educators, and other stakeholders. If these groups operate in silos, with limited communication and understanding of each other's perspectives, it becomes difficult to build consensus and drive meaningful reform.

To overcome these challenges, a thorough review of the current system is urgently needed. This review should involve a critical examination of the existing policies, regulations, and power structures that hinder innovation and autonomy in higher education. It should also include a comprehensive analysis of best practices from other countries, particularly those with highly successful and competitive university systems.

Based on this review, a comprehensive set of countermeasures should be developed and implemented. These measures should address the root causes of resistance to change, promote greater autonomy for universities, and foster a culture of innovation and continuous improvement in higher education.

Only through a concerted effort involving all stakeholders—policymakers, educators, students, and the broader community—can we hope to overcome the obstacles to educational reform and create a truly world-class higher education system in South Korea.

Heungseon Daewongun turned Joseon into a hermit kingdom

As this book will discuss in the rise and fall of human civilization, for thousands of years from before the Common Era until the 16th century, China's level of science and technology (e.g., the invention of paper, printing, the compass, and gunpowder) was far ahead of that of the West.

However, strangely, the 17th century's "Scientific Revolution" and "Industrial Revolution" began not in China, which had led the world in scientific and technological advancement, but in Europe, which had acquired and developed information about Chinese science and technology.

Why has the West dominated modern human civilization (military power, economic power, science and technology, humanities, etc.) for over 300 years?

Throughout its long history, China has been a vast and influential civilization, often dwarfing its neighbors in both size and cultural development. This sense of scale, coupled with a deeply ingrained Sinocentric worldview, shaped China's perception of its place in the world. The Chinese believed their civilization to be the center of the Earth, the pinnacle of human achievement, and the rightful leader of all nations.

Given China's immense size and the relative lack of development in other parts of the world before the 17th century, the question of whether to maintain open or closed borders was not a pressing concern for the Chinese. Their self-sufficiency and sense of cultural superiority fostered a degree of isolationism. There was little incentive to actively engage with other civilizations, as they believed that the world naturally gravitated towards China.

Indeed, China's history unfolded without a pressing need to reach beyond its borders. While the Chinese people largely remained within their own territory, people from other civilizations actively sought out China, bringing their knowledge, goods, and cultural practices to the Middle Kingdom. They often paid tribute to the Chinese emperors and sought to learn from the advanced civilization that they perceived China to be.

This dynamic reinforced China's Sinocentric worldview and contributed to a sense of complacency. The influx of foreign envoys and tribute bearers reinforced the belief that China was the center of the world, reducing the perceived need for outward engagement and exploration. This inward focus, while understandable in its historical context, may have ultimately contributed to China's relative decline in the face of the Scientific Revolution and the Industrial Revolution that transformed the West.

Even after the 17th century, when the Scientific Revolution and Industrial Revolution began to transform the West, China clung to its Sinocentric worldview. The belief in China's cultural and intellectual superiority persisted, leading to a growing indifference towards exchange and communication with other civilizations. This inward focus was further reinforced by the enduring influence of

Confucianism, with its emphasis on tradition and social harmony, and a bureaucratic system that valued stability and conformity.

As the world entered the modern era, science and technology emerged as the driving forces behind national power and economic prosperity. The nature of warfare underwent a dramatic transformation, shifting from battles fought with swords and spears to conflicts dominated by guns, cannons, and tanks. The West, fueled by its embrace of scientific inquiry and technological innovation, led this transformation, establishing its dominance on the global stage.

China, meanwhile, struggled to adapt to these rapid changes. Its closed-off approach to the outside world limited its access to new knowledge and technologies, leaving it vulnerable to external pressures and internal stagnation. From the 17th to the 20th centuries, China suffered greatly as the West surged ahead in various fields, including food production, medicine, agriculture, and infrastructure.

This period of relative decline can be attributed, in part, to China's reluctance to engage with the outside world and embrace new ideas. The consequences of maintaining closed borders and clinging to outdated paradigms were significant, hindering China's progress and leaving it vulnerable to exploitation by Western powers.

While China has experienced remarkable economic growth and development under its recent socialist system with a market-oriented economy, questions remain about its long-term trajectory. The challenges of balancing economic growth with social stability, environmental sustainability, and individual freedoms remain significant. Whether China can fully embrace openness and adapt to the complexities of the 21st century will ultimately determine its future success.

As China's per capita income rises and its socialist system undergoes further transformations, predicting its future trajectory becomes increasingly complex. While economic prosperity can bring many benefits, it can also lead to new challenges and unforeseen consequences. Some observers express concerns about the sustainability of China's current model, given its reliance on export-driven growth, its growing income inequality, and its environmental challenges.

However, history provides valuable lessons about the importance of openness for national development. For centuries, China's Sinocentric worldview and relative isolation limited its engagement with the outside world. This inward focus, while understandable in its historical context, may have ultimately hindered China's progress and contributed to its relative decline in the face of Western advancements.

To achieve sustainable development and maintain its upward trajectory, China must embrace a more open and interconnected approach. This involves actively engaging in exchange and communication with other civilizations, learning from their experiences, and sharing its own knowledge and innovations with the world.

By fostering a culture of openness and collaboration, China can tap into the vast potential of the global knowledge economy, attract talent and investment, and contribute to solving global challenges.

This outward-looking approach can also help to counterbalance the potential risks associated with rapid economic growth and social change.

While the future of China remains uncertain, one thing is clear: embracing openness and actively engaging with the global community will be crucial for its continued success. Joseon (朝鮮), the last kingdom of Korea, traversed a complex path of interaction and isolation with the outside world. There were periods of openness, such as when Arab merchants frequented its shores, bringing with them new goods and ideas. Later, Western civilization also made its presence known, knocking on Joseon's door with increasing persistence.

However, whether due to fear of the unknown, a desire to preserve its cultural identity, or a rigid adherence to Confucian principles, Joseon never fully embraced openness. During the reign of Heungseon Daewongun(興宣大院君) in the 19th century, the country entered a period of strict isolationism, closing its doors even tighter to external influences. This isolationist stance exemplifies the characteristics of a closed system, where interaction with the outside world is limited, and the flow of information and innovation is restricted.

In contrast, Japan, an island nation with a history of openness to foreign influences, adopted a different approach. A century earlier than Korea, Japan had already opened its borders and actively embraced the advancements of Western civilization. This proactive engagement with the outside world allowed Japan to rapidly modernize and strengthen its military and economic power.

The consequences of Joseon's isolationism were profound. The Imjin War(壬辰倭亂) in the late 16th century, where Japan invaded Korea, exposed the vulnerabilities of a closed system. Joseon suffered a humiliating defeat, and decades later, it fell under Japanese colonial rule, a period of national hardship and oppression.

Even today, the legacy of this historical interaction continues to shape the relationship between Korea and Japan. Disputes over Dokdo Island, Japanese politicians' visits to the Yasukuni Shrine, and the unresolved issue of forced labor during wartime continue to strain relations between the two countries.

While it's easy to criticize Japan's actions and harbor resentment for past wrongs, closing our borders, both physically and mentally, is not a viable solution. Instead, we must learn from history and embrace a more open and strategic approach. By engaging with the world, learning from others, and cultivating our own strengths, we can navigate the complexities of the 21st century and ensure a prosperous and secure future for Korea.

North Korea stands as a stark example of the perils of isolationism in the modern world. For decades, it has maintained a rigid closed system, sealing its borders and strictly limiting the flow of information, people, and goods. This self-imposed isolation has had devastating consequences.

North Korea's economy has teetered on the brink of collapse for decades, leaving its people facing unimaginable hardships. Food shortages, limited access to essential goods and services, and a repressive political system have created a humanitarian crisis that demands attention.

While the situation in North Korea may seem like a distant problem, it serves as a potent reminder of the interconnectedness of our world. The suffering of the North Korean people should resonate with us all, prompting us to reflect on the importance of compassion, cooperation, and the pursuit of a more just and equitable world.

If North Korea's leaders were to embrace a more open approach, the country's future could be dramatically different. By opening its borders, engaging in dialogue with the international community, and allowing for the free flow of information and ideas, North Korea could begin to address its economic challenges, improve the lives of its citizens, and contribute to regional stability.

In the 21st century, where globalization and technological advancements have blurred national boundaries, openness is no longer a choice but a necessity for progress and prosperity. History has repeatedly demonstrated that isolationism leads to stagnation, decline, and ultimately, suffering. No nation or society can thrive in a vacuum.

The North Korean issue is not just a regional concern; it is a global challenge that calls for collective action and a renewed commitment to the principles of openness, cooperation, and human dignity. By working together to foster a more open and interconnected world, we can create a brighter future for all, including the long-suffering people of North Korea.

An open system is the foundation upon which convergence, integration, and open innovation can thrive

Scientists today face a unique set of challenges. In addition to the inherent complexities of their chosen fields, they are increasingly expected to venture beyond the traditional confines of science and engage with the humanities, social sciences, and even the arts. The buzzwords of "convergence" and "integration" are everywhere, reflecting a growing recognition that knowledge creation and problem-solving in the 21st century require a more holistic and interdisciplinary approach.

While this trend may seem daunting to some, it also presents exciting opportunities. By venturing beyond the silos of their specialized disciplines, scientists can gain new perspectives, discover unexpected connections, and contribute to a richer and more nuanced understanding of the world.

The notion that science and the humanities are separate domains is a relatively recent phenomenon. Throughout history, many of the greatest thinkers seamlessly integrated knowledge from various fields. Leonardo da Vinci, for example, was not only a brilliant artist but also a skilled engineer, inventor, and anatomist. His interdisciplinary approach allowed him to make groundbreaking contributions in a wide range of fields.

In the past, the boundaries between academic disciplines were

more fluid, allowing scholars to roam freely across different domains of knowledge. This fostered a more holistic and integrated approach to scholarship, leading to deeper insights and a broader understanding of the human condition.

Today, as specialization has become the norm, it's easy to lose sight of the interconnectedness of knowledge. However, all academic disciplines ultimately serve the same purpose: to advance human understanding and improve our world. Physics, for example, doesn't exist in a vacuum. Its principles and discoveries have profound implications for other fields, from engineering and medicine to philosophy and art.

To truly contribute to the betterment of humanity, scientists must embrace an open system of academia, where collaboration and cross-pollination of ideas are encouraged. This requires a willingness to step outside one's comfort zone, engage with different perspectives, and recognize the value of diverse approaches to knowledge creation. By fostering a spirit of openness and interdisciplinary collaboration, we can unlock new possibilities for innovation and create a more holistic and integrated understanding of the world around us.

Yukawa Hideki, the renowned Japanese physicist who won the Nobel Prize in Physics in 1949, attributed his groundbreaking work to an unlikely source: classical Chinese literature. He credited his deep familiarity with the works of Li Bai(李白) and Zhuangzi(莊子), fostered by his family's intellectual environment, for sparking the inspiration that led to his meson theory.

From a young age, Yukawa immersed himself in the rich world of Chinese classics, including the Four Books and Tang Dynasty poetry. Surprisingly, it was within these poetic verses that he found the seeds of his scientific breakthrough. The philosophical ideas and imaginative imagery of these texts, particularly the works of Li Bai, expanded his thinking and allowed him to approach scientific problems from a unique perspective.

Li Bai, a renowned poet of the Tang Dynasty, possessed a remarkable ability to evoke the vastness of the cosmos and the ephemeral nature of human existence. His verses often conveyed a sense of awe and wonder at the natural world, capturing the interconnectedness of all things and the insignificance of human affairs in the grand scheme of the universe.

It's as if Li Bai had peered into the depths of the cosmos, transcending the limitations of his earthly perspective. His poems evoke images of soaring through the heavens, gazing upon the Earth as a mere grain of sand in the vast expanse of the universe. This cosmic perspective, so vividly expressed in his poetry, resonates with modern astrophysics and our understanding of the universe's immensity.

Yukawa's story reminds us that inspiration can come from unexpected sources. By cultivating a broad intellectual curiosity and engaging with diverse fields of knowledge, we can open our minds to new possibilities and discover connections that might otherwise remain hidden. The boundaries between science and the humanities are not as rigid as we might think. In fact, it is often at the intersection of these disciplines that the most profound insights and breakthroughs emerge.

In recent years, a growing emphasis on convergence and interdisciplinary thinking has emerged, not just in academia but across society as a whole. The traditional model of valuing deep expertise in a single, narrow field is gradually giving way to a recognition that innovation and progress often arise from the integration of knowledge and skills from diverse domains.

This shift is evident in the countless examples of individuals who have achieved breakthroughs by crossing disciplinary boundaries. Steve Jobs, the visionary behind Apple, famously combined his understanding of technology with a keen sense of design and aesthetics, revolutionizing the consumer electronics industry. Similarly, Nobel laureate physicist Yukawa Hideki drew inspiration from classical Chinese literature to develop his groundbreaking meson theory.

The interconnectedness of knowledge is undeniable. A discovery in one field can often have profound implications for others. This is only natural, considering that all academic disciplines are ultimately products of human inquiry and share a common goal: to understand and improve the world around us.

However, in today's increasingly specialized world, it's easy to become trapped within the confines of a single discipline. Many individuals focus solely on their area of expertise, neglecting the broader landscape of knowledge and the potential for cross-pollination of ideas. This overspecialization can limit creativity, hinder innovation, and leave individuals vulnerable to disruption when their narrow field of expertise becomes obsolete.

By venturing beyond the boundaries of our specialized knowledge, we can gain new perspectives, overcome obstacles that may seem insurmountable within a single discipline, and even create entirely new fields of inquiry through the harmonious integration of diverse ideas.

To achieve this, we need to cultivate an open awareness of the broader world and an active attitude of challenging our assumptions and exploring new possibilities. We must embrace the spirit of lifelong learning, constantly seeking new knowledge and connections, and recognizing that the most profound insights often emerge at the intersection of disciplines. By fostering a culture of interdisciplinary collaboration and embracing the principles of open systems, we can unlock our full potential for innovation and create a more dynamic and interconnected world.

Fusion(融合, 융합) can be likened to a chemical reaction, where different elements combine to create something entirely new. The Chinese character "融" (yung), meaning "to melt" or "to fuse," beautifully captures this concept. It depicts a cauldron with three legs (鬲) and an insect (虫), symbolizing the steam rising like an insect from the lid of a boiling cauldron. This imagery evokes the transformation that occurs when disparate elements merge and blend, losing their individual identities to form a new substance.

Just as hydrogen and oxygen, two distinct elements, combine to create water, a substance with entirely different properties, convergence involves the fusion of diverse ideas, disciplines, or technologies to generate novel solutions and innovations. If we cling to our existing knowledge and perspectives, we limit our potential for progress. Convergence is the catalyst that allows us to transcend these limitations and create something truly new.

While convergence involves the fusion of elements, integration is more akin to a dialogue or collaboration between different domains. It's the process of communication and exchange that allows seemingly disparate fields to inform and enrich one another. The meeting of philosophy and architecture, the interplay between art and music, or the integration of technology and healthcare are all examples of this dynamic interplay.

However, both convergence and integration require a crucial prerequisite: an open system mindset. This involves a willingness to break down existing boundaries, challenge assumptions, and embrace new perspectives. Without this spirit of openness, neither convergence, integration, nor open innovation can truly flourish.

An open system fosters an environment where ideas can flow freely, where cross-pollination between disciplines is encouraged, and where individuals are empowered to explore the uncharted territories of knowledge and creativity. It is within this fertile ground of openness that the seeds of convergence and integration can take root and blossom, leading to transformative breakthroughs and a more interconnected and dynamic world.

Scientists should no longer be confined to the isolation of their laboratories, surrounded by equations and experimental apparatus. They should venture beyond the traditional boundaries of their discipline, seeking inspiration and insight from unexpected sources. They should read natural science in the evocative language of literature, discovering the laws of thermodynamics in the rhythmic cycles of poetry, and uncovering the secrets of the cosmos in the harmonious melodies of music.

By cultivating an open-system spirit that transcends disciplinary boundaries, scientists can become truly well-rounded intellectuals. They can develop a deeper understanding of the human condition, appreciate the interconnectedness of knowledge, and contribute to a more holistic and integrated vision of the world.

This openness to diverse perspectives and experiences can spark creativity, fuel innovation, and lead to unexpected breakthroughs. When scientists engage with the humanities, the arts, and the social sciences, they gain new tools and frameworks for understanding the complex challenges facing our world. They can develop more nuanced and effective solutions that consider not only the scientific aspects of a problem but also its social, ethical, and cultural dimensions.

In an era of increasing specialization, it's more important than ever for scientists to embrace a broader perspective. By cultivating an open-system spirit, they can become catalysts for change, bridging the gap between science and society and contributing to a more just, sustainable, and enlightened world.

Ven. Beopjeong was a true leader of an open system

The teachings of Ven. Beopjeong (法頂) Sunim, a revered Buddhist monk and spiritual leader, have profoundly influenced my understanding of non-possession (無所有). His philosophy, rooted in the Buddhist principle of non-attachment, emphasizes the liberation that comes from releasing our clinging to material possessions and worldly desires.

I often contemplate the connection between non-possession and the concept of boundarylessness (無經界). When we let go of our attachment to possessions, we free ourselves from the limitations they impose. Just as breaking free from physical or mental boundaries expands our horizons and opens us to new possibilities, so too does non-attachment liberate us from the constraints of desire and the illusion of ownership.

In a society driven by consumerism and the relentless pursuit of material wealth, the philosophy of non-possession offers a radical paradigm shift. It challenges us to redefine our values and find contentment in simplicity and gratitude. This shift, while seemingly counterintuitive, can lead to a profound sense of freedom and inner peace.

By releasing our attachment to possessions, we recognize that everything we truly need already exists in abundance in the natural world. We are part of a vast and interconnected ecosystem, and the resources we require for sustenance and well-being are readily available to us.

Instead of striving to possess a small patch of nature in the form of a manicured garden, we can embrace the entire forest as our own. The trees, the flowers, the flowing streams-all become part of our extended garden, a shared space of beauty and tranquility.

This perspective, where we recognize the interconnectedness of all things and relinquish our desire for individual ownership, aligns with the philosophy of non-possession and the concept of boundarylessness. It is a world where we can both possess and not possess, where we are both connected and free. It is a world of abundance, where our needs are met, and our spirits are nourished by the beauty and generosity of the natural world.

Beopjeong Sunim exemplified the spirit of openness and interconnectivity that I believe is essential for personal and societal growth. He was not confined by the boundaries of his own Buddhist faith but actively sought dialogue and understanding with those of other religions. He engaged in meaningful conversations with Catholic priests and nuns, Protestant pastors, and scholars from various traditions.

This open-mindedness stands in stark contrast to the more insular tendencies often found within organized religion. Many religious institutions and individuals adhere to a rigid set of beliefs and practices, viewing their own faith as the sole path to salvation. This exclusivity can create closed systems that stifle dialogue, foster intolerance, and hinder progress.

The notion that those who do not adhere to a particular creed are destined for eternal damnation is a prime example of such a closed system. It creates artificial boundaries that divide people and promote conflict rather than understanding.

Beopjeong Sunim, however, transcended these limitations. He recognized the inherent value in all spiritual traditions and sought common ground through dialogue and mutual respect. He embodied the spirit of an open system, where boundaries are fluid, and the free exchange of ideas is encouraged.

His willingness to engage with diverse perspectives and learn from those with different beliefs makes him a true role model for open-mindedness and interfaith understanding. He dared to challenge the rigid boundaries that often define religious discourse, demonstrating that true spirituality lies in embracing compassion, empathy, and a willingness to connect with others across lines of difference.

Beopjeong Sunim's legacy serves as a powerful reminder that openness is not just a philosophical concept; it is a way of being that can transform individuals, communities, and even the world. By embracing the principles of open systems, we can create a more inclusive, harmonious, and enlightened world where everyone has the opportunity to thrive.

Beopjeong Sunim's life serves as a powerful example of how the principles of open systems can be applied to personal growth and spiritual development. While he maintained an open boundary in his interactions with the world, his exchange of material goods and cultural influences was strikingly asymmetrical.

He consciously limited the inflow of material possessions, embracing a life of simplicity and frugality. He had few personal belongings and lived in a modest hermitage, demonstrating a deep understanding of the Buddhist principle of non-attachment.

However, when it came to the outflow of his spiritual wisdom and teachings, he was incredibly generous. He shared his insights through countless essays, lectures, and public talks, touching the lives of millions and inspiring them to seek a more meaningful and fulfilling existence.

This asymmetry reflects a profound wisdom: to truly enrich the world, one must first empty oneself of worldly desires and attachments. Beopjeong Sunim embodied this principle, discarding material pursuits and focusing on cultivating inner peace and spiritual growth.

He lived a life deeply connected to nature, finding beauty and truth in the simplicity of the natural world. Like a blade of grass, he swayed gently in the winds of life, offering his wisdom and compassion to all who crossed his path.

Beopjeong Sunim's legacy is a testament to the transformative power of non-possession and openness. By releasing our attachment to material things and embracing a spirit of generosity and interconnectedness, we can create a richer and more meaningful life for ourselves and for others.

Beopjeong Sunim's commitment to a life of simplicity and spiritual richness is powerfully illustrated by the few possessions he left behind in his Suyu Sanbang(수유산방) retreat in Odaesan, Gangwon-do. After his passing, it was discovered that his worldly belongings consisted of only a few books, an old radio that brought him the joy of music, a simple teacup, and a small vegetable garden where he cultivated his own food.

These meager possessions speak volumes about his detachment from material things and his profound understanding of the Buddhist principle of non-possession. He lived a life free from the clutter of worldly desires, focusing instead on cultivating inner peace and spiritual growth.

Despite his physically secluded lifestyle, Beopjeong Sunim's boundaries, both personal and spiritual, were infinitely open. He embraced the world with an open heart, engaging in dialogue with people from all walks of life and sharing his wisdom generously.

He discarded the superfluous and embraced the essential, creating a life of profound simplicity and meaning. He exemplified the concept of an open system, demonstrating that true fulfillment comes not from accumulating possessions but from cultivating inner richness and connecting with the world in a meaningful way.

Beopjeong Sunim's legacy serves as an inspiration to us all. He reminds us that true freedom lies in letting go of our attachments and embracing a life of openness, generosity, and interconnectedness. By following his example, we can cultivate a deeper sense of purpose, find joy in simplicity, and contribute to a more compassionate and harmonious world.

Chapter 2

Implementation of an Open System

The creative ability that is valued in this new era requires more than just the ability to propose solutions that others cannot think of. It demands a 'unique insight'.
This includes the ability to clearly identify the 'essence of a problem' in a complex reality, to redefine the essence of a problem in a new and different way, and to concretize seemingly absurd ideas into feasible ones.

- Jae-Seung Chung

Beyond boundaries: Innovation through Openness

Open-Minded Person!
Open World!

You can find open systems everywhere,
from schools to history to whole countries.
I think South Korean young people should take
a look at the Netherlands.
It's a great example of an open society.
 A place where everyone speaks multiple languages
and is always up for a challenge.
That's the kind of future I hope for our youth.

The Open system of academia

Take cross-disciplinary courses between the humanities and sciences

Universities should be vibrant hubs of intellectual exploration, where curiosity knows no bounds. Students should be encouraged to venture beyond the confines of their chosen majors and delve into the rich tapestry of human knowledge. It is through this cross-pollination of ideas and perspectives that true innovation and understanding emerge.

The notion that one should remain solely within their own field of study, ignorant of others, is a disservice to the very spirit of academia. All disciplines are interconnected, weaving together a complex and fascinating web of knowledge. To close oneself off, believing that one's own field is the only valid or valuable one, is to limit one's intellectual growth and potential for discovery.

Consider the Renaissance polymath Leonardo da Vinci, a master of art, science, and engineering. His insatiable curiosity led him to explore a vast range of subjects, from painting and sculpture to anatomy, botany, and mechanics. Similarly, the Joseon-era scholar Jeong Yak-yong(丁若鏞), renowned for his architectural achievements, also made significant contributions to civil engineering, mechanics, and cartography.

These intellectual giants did not confine themselves to a single field of study. They followed their curiosity wherever it led, crossing disciplinary boundaries with ease and drawing inspiration from diverse sources. This open-minded approach to learning allowed them to make groundbreaking contributions in a multitude of fields.

Even in my own undergraduate years, as an engineering student, I felt the pull of other disciplines. I would occasionally audit courses in poetry creation and English literature, finding that these experiences broadened my perspective and enriched my understanding of the world. My mind, which had been focused solely on the technicalities of engineering, felt liberated and invigorated by these forays into the humanities.

This is the true essence of an open academic system—a system that encourages intellectual curiosity, fosters interdisciplinary exploration, and empowers students to become well-rounded

individuals with a broad and nuanced understanding of the world.

Upon entering university, students should resist the temptation to confine themselves solely to their chosen major. Even those pursuing humanities degrees should consider venturing into the realms of science and technology, exploring subjects like biology, computer science, or architecture. Similarly, science and engineering students can benefit greatly from immersing themselves in the humanities, arts, and social sciences.

In today's world, with its abundance of educational resources and technological tools, the pursuit of knowledge is no longer limited to the confines of the classroom. Anyone with a thirst for learning can access a vast array of information and educational materials, regardless of their background or location.

If time constraints are a concern, there are countless ways to integrate learning into your daily routine. Educational apps, online courses, and podcasts offer the flexibility to learn at your own pace and convenience.

For example, I often utilize my commute time to listen to lectures from SEBASI (세바시), a popular Korean online platform that features insightful talks on a wide range of topics. Similar to TED Talks, SEBASI offers a diverse collection of lectures by experts in various fields, providing a stimulating and thought-provoking way to learn and expand one's horizons.

By embracing these opportunities for lifelong learning and cultivating a curious and open mind, we can continually grow, adapt, and thrive in an ever-changing world.

It's a concerning statistic: reportedly, half of South Korean adults majored in the humanities and have limited interest in scientific fields, resulting in a level of science knowledge equivalent to that of a middle school student. This disregard for science among humanities students is a significant issue that needs to be addressed.

University students, regardless of their chosen major, should possess a solid foundation in basic scientific principles. Science is not merely a collection of facts and formulas; it's a way of understanding the world, a framework for critical thinking, and a driving force behind human progress.

Park Mun-ho, a prominent advocate for science education, argues that 80% of human knowledge originates from natural science. He emphasizes the importance of a balanced education that includes both the humanities and the sciences, suggesting an 8:2 ratio in favor of science for intellectuals.

While this ratio may seem skewed towards science, it underscores a crucial point: science plays a fundamental role in shaping our understanding of the world and driving human advancement. From the development of medicine and technology to the exploration of the cosmos and the understanding of our own biology, science has profoundly impacted the course of human history.

Dismissing science simply because it's not one's primary field of study limits our intellectual growth and prevents us from fully appreciating the interconnectedness of knowledge. A well-rounded education should encompass both the humanities and the sciences, fostering a deeper understanding of the human condition and the world around us.

By embracing a more balanced approach to learning, we can

cultivate critical thinking skills, expand our perspectives, and become more informed and engaged citizens. We can also gain a greater appreciation for the remarkable achievements of science and its potential to address the challenges facing humanity in the 21st century.

We often categorize the study of humans as the humanities and the study of nature as the natural sciences. But is this division truly accurate? Are humans and nature truly separate entities, or are we inextricably intertwined, part of a single, interconnected whole?

Perhaps the limitations we impose on our understanding of the world stem from this artificial dichotomy. By creating rigid boundaries between disciplines, we confine our thinking and limit our potential for discovery. Dichotomies, by their very nature, create closed systems that restrict the free flow of ideas and perspectives.

This tendency to categorize and compartmentalize knowledge extends beyond academia. We see it in the political sphere, where the labels of "progressivism" and "conservatism" often create rigid ideological divides. Once trapped within these confines, our perspectives narrow, and our ability to engage in meaningful dialogue diminishes.

Even in education, where the separation of humanities and sciences has long been the norm, we are witnessing a growing recognition of the value of interdisciplinary studies. However, to truly embrace this trend, we must move beyond simply adding a few cross-listed courses to the curriculum. We must fundamentally challenge the belief that knowledge can be neatly compartmentalized into distinct domains.

Humanities students should not shy away from exploring the wonders of the natural world through books like Carl Sagan's Cosmos. Engineering students should cultivate an appreciation for literature and the arts, carrying a novel or two alongside their textbooks. Science books are infused with human passion, curiosity, and creativity, while novels often delve into the complexities of human nature and the social implications of scientific progress.

It is by freely traversing these artificial boundaries, by embracing the interconnectedness of knowledge, that we can become truly well-rounded intellectuals. We can develop a deeper understanding of ourselves, our world, and our place within the grand tapestry of existence.

I recently encountered a graduate student majoring in business administration who expressed a sentiment I've heard echoed by many others. They lamented the lack of interdisciplinary programs and educational opportunities that bridge the gap between the humanities and the sciences in Korea. They felt frustrated by the perceived lack of support within public educational institutions and the expectation that individuals must shoulder the burden of seeking out such knowledge independently.

While I empathize with this student's frustration, I also believe that their perception of limited opportunities may be overly pessimistic. The doors to interdisciplinary learning are not as firmly shut as they might appear. With a bit of initiative and a willingness to explore, a world of knowledge awaits.

The world of science, often perceived as intimidating or inaccessible to those with a humanities background, is filled with wonder and beauty. Why not venture into an engineering classroom and witness firsthand the creative process of designing and building solutions to real-world problems? Or pick up a classic science book, like Carl Sagan's Cosmos, and embark on a journey through the vast expanse of the universe, guided by a master storyteller.

Open systems reveal themselves to those who actively seek them out. The pursuit of knowledge is not a passive endeavor; it requires curiosity, a willingness to step outside one's comfort zone, and a proactive approach to learning. By embracing this spirit of inquiry, we can unlock the interconnectedness of knowledge and discover the hidden pathways that link seemingly disparate disciplines.

The boundaries between the humanities and the sciences are not insurmountable. With a bit of effort and an open mind, we can all become explorers in the vast landscape of human knowledge, discovering new connections, expanding our horizons, and enriching our understanding of the world.

The Silk Road and The Travels of Marco Polo: An Open Encounter Between East and West

"A lady from the Western Regions, with curly hair and blue eyes,

plays music in a quiet night-time tavern.

The sound is as if it were descending from heaven,

but beneath the bright moon,

she gazes towards her homeland and weeps endlessly."

This verse from a poem written 1,300 years ago by the Tang Dynasty poet Li He (李賀) speaks volumes about the human experiences intertwined with the Silk Road. The "lady from the Western Regions" likely refers to a huqi (胡姬), a foreign woman who worked in a tavern in Chang'an (長安), the capital of the Tang Dynasty. Chang'an was a cosmopolitan hub during this period, drawing merchants, travelers, and scholars from across Eurasia. This verse not only captures the presence of diverse cultures in Tang China but also hints at the complexities of such encounters, including the woman's apparent longing for home amidst the beauty of her music. This is but one anecdote illustrating the movement of people and cultures back and forth between the East and West along the Silk Road, a testament to the enduring human connections forged through this ancient network.

The Silk Road was a transformative phenomenon that revolutionized contact between East and West. While exchange existed before, the Silk Road significantly opened up interaction and facilitated unprecedented levels of cultural exchange. The term "Silk Road" itself emerged in the 19th century, coined by the German geographer Ferdinand von Richthofen (1833–1905). This intricate network of routes fostered the exchange of goods and ideas between East and West. Through the Silk Road, elements of Islamic civilization, such as [specific examples, e.g., scientific knowledge, architectural styles], spread, leading to changes in [specific regions or cultures]. In this way, the East and West met, shared, and merged, enriching each other's cultures.

The Silk Road facilitated significant cultural exchange. However, Europe's response to Islamic civilization during the Middle Ages was complex. It varied across different regions and time periods. There were instances of conflict and hostility, such as the Crusades. But it's important to remember that Europe was not a single entity. Some regions experienced considerable intellectual exchange with Islamic cultures. They readily absorbed Islamic knowledge, particularly in science and philosophy.

However, there were also signs of closed-mindedness. Some were reluctant to fully embrace the contributions of other civilizations. The historian Henri Pirenne argued that European civilization was deeply influenced by Islamic civilization. He believed that European civilization might not have developed as it did without this influence. This highlights how important openness and exchange are for progress. Arrogance and isolation can hinder a society's development. But a willingness to learn from other cultures encourages growth and innovation.

Marco Polo played a crucial role in transforming the perceptions and interactions between East and West. In 1271, he embarked on a long journey to the East with his father and uncle, who were jewel merchants. Departing from Venice, he crossed the Black Sea. He traversed the Pamir Plateau and the Tarim Basin. Finally, he arrived in Beijing, the capital of the Yuan Dynasty, where Kublai Khan ruled.

The young merchant gained Kublai Khan's trust and served in various administrative positions in China from 1275 to 1292. During this time, he became deeply familiar with Chinese civilization. His experiences provided him with unique insights into the East, which he later shared with the West.

In 1292, Marco Polo departed from Quanzhou, the largest trading port in southern China. He sailed through the South China Sea, the Strait of Malacca, the Indian Ocean, the Arabian Sea, and the Persian Gulf, finally returning to his homeland in 1295. His accounts of his travels introduced Europeans to the wonders and complexities of the East, contributing to a greater understanding and exchange between the two worlds.

In truth, Marco Polo was just one traveler among many. We don't need to exaggerate his importance. However, the records of his journeys had a profound impact on Europe.

His book, The Travels, opened up the East to European imaginations. One reader, Christopher Columbus, was so captivated by Marco Polo's descriptions of China that he underlined passages in the book. This sparked Columbus's curiosity, and he decided to embark on his own journey to the East.

This illustrates how open systems create more open systems. They inspire new ideas and actions. In contrast, closed systems stagnate and ultimately fade away.

Marco Polo's travels, and their impact on people like Columbus, show how even a single journey can spark great changes in the world.

The Silk Road and accounts like The Travels of Marco Polo fostered connections between East and West. However, it's important to also acknowledge the role of conflict in driving interaction throughout history.

War, despite its devastating consequences, often forces contact between different cultures. Take the Mongol conquests, for example. They led to a widespread exchange of goods, ideas, and technologies across Eurasia. Similarly, the Crusades, though violent, brought European and Middle Eastern civilizations into close contact.

This exchange, however, is often unequal and filled with violence. It's debatable whether war can truly be considered an "open system," as it frequently involves domination and the suppression of one culture by another.

Yet, it's undeniable that war has sometimes broken down barriers, leading to the transmission of ideas and technologies, albeit in a tragic and destructive way. This highlights the complex nature of cultural exchange, where even the darkest chapters of human history can have unintended consequences.

History shows us that open systems often emerge through cultural exchanges, travel, and even war. Ultimately, it's about trying something new – a willingness to embrace new experiences and engage with different cultures. This is what shapes the course of history.

Our youth should not be passive observers. They should actively seek out new experiences, for their own sake and the future of humanity. This could involve learning a new language, traveling to unfamiliar places, or engaging with people from different backgrounds.

These actions, however small they may seem, contribute to building a more open and interconnected world. No one can predict their full impact. An open system is a realm of infinite possibilities, where even the smallest actions can lead to unforeseen and transformative outcomes.

The Open System of a Nation

Netherlands, the country of Guus Hiddink, is a representative open system

I love Dutch football because it's so aggressive. While it might be a stretch to infer a nation's character solely from its football style, I do think the Dutch people share that aggressive spirit. Remember when coach Guus Hiddink, after leading South Korea to the semifinals of the 2002 World Cup, said they were still hungry for more? That's the Dutch mentality! The Netherlands is a country that isn't afraid of failure and is always trying new things. It's a prime example of an open society that aggressively breaks down closed systems.

Despite being a small country in Europe, the Netherlands has become a powerful nation that rivals Germany and France. But geographically, the Netherlands isn't blessed with the best land. Located in the lower reaches of the Rhine, it's prone to floods and affected by North Sea storms.

While other European powers like England, Spain, and Portugal were exploring the unknown world by sea in the 15th century, the Dutch were busy fighting those floods and storms. To survive in this harsh environment, young people had to build dikes and dams.

Once they successfully constructed these defenses, the Dutch were the last in Europe to venture out to sea. And when they did, they did so with a vengeance! At that time, 1 million out of a population of 2 million became sailors, demonstrating their boldness and aggression.

With an open mindset, the entire nation challenged themselves. They ventured out into the world. This led them to establish the Dutch East India Company. It was the world's largest maritime trading company at the time.

I hope that young people in my country, Korea, can learn from the open-mindedness of the Dutch. The Dutch people are optimistic and open-minded. They exhibit a positive attitude, friendliness, and a spirit of compromise. The Netherlands is even more of a free-market economy than the United States, a country often associated with individualism. They've even legalized controversial issues like homosexuality, drugs, and prostitution as a counterintuitive way to prevent problems.

One of the things we can learn from the Dutch is language.

Perhaps out of necessity to survive, many Dutch people are multilingual. It's common to find Dutch citizens who are fluent in French, German, and English. As we know, Guus Hiddink is said to speak five languages. It is reported that 72% of Dutch CEOs are trilingual. Ninety percent of the population speaks at least one foreign language. 44% speak two, and 12% speak three.

Despite having fewer language schools, the Dutch feel confident in their foreign language abilities. University students gain international experience in neighboring countries and acquire considerable foreign language skills. I believe that language is the most important key to creating an open system. Once you acquire a language, you can showcase your abilities anywhere in the world and absorb global knowledge. In this sense, the Netherlands can be considered a prime example of an open system.

The more I delve into the Netherlands, the more fascinating I find it. It was the first country to convert military aircraft into passenger planes. In 1919, the Netherlands established the world's first airline, introducing first-class and economy class seating. They've transformed their frozen winter dams into skating rinks. And because of their history of dealing with floods and storms, swimming has become a mandatory subject for children. The abundance of famous Dutch swimmers and cyclists is a testament to this.

I've met Dutch people before and was really impressed by their considerate nature. I've heard that the Dutch never resort to physical violence. I can't confirm this, but based on my limited interactions, I'm inclined to believe it.

Dutch children have a very strong sense of economics. They clean their old toys, dolls, bicycles, and recyclables and sell them at a flea market for a reasonable price. This is what a Dutch flea market is all about. And this is what an open system looks like for Dutch children. They find great joy and excitement in dealing directly with their peers. And even though the income is small, they develop a sense of self-reliance. If I want to effectively convey the concept of an open system to young people in South Korea, I would start by telling them to learn from the Dutch.

The open system of science

The God particle, Higgs, which opens the invisible

What is this world, this universe, made of? It's a question humanity has pondered for millennia, one that remains unanswered. Some say water, others fire. Water, air, fire, earth… but we can't definitively say that these elements alone created the world. Science judges only what is visible. It doesn't acknowledge the invisible or the unprovable. That which is unacknowledged is a closed system.

Scientists must also have open minds to discover new values. The belief that something can only be true if it can be experimentally proven is a closed-minded approach and a closed system. That said, it's not about blindly believing in unproven things.

Scientists have made countless efforts to prove what the world is made of. As a result, modern physicists have proposed the Standard Model, which explains natural phenomena based on quantum physics. These scientists claim that there are 17 fundamental particles that make up all matter in the universe and the forces that govern it. This Standard Model is composed of six quarks, six leptons, four force-carrying particles, and the Higgs boson, which gives mass to these particles. These 17 particles are the fundamental building blocks of all matter and forces in nature.

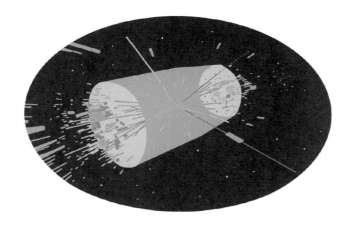

Yet, while all other particles except the Higgs had been found, the final piece, the Higgs boson, proved elusive. Finding it would complete the Standard Model and validate all the scientific theories that had come before. The Higgs boson is an invisible particle that gives mass to all things and then disappears. The theory is that all matter is composed of 16 particles and this Higgs boson.

Although its existence was theoretically sound, actually finding the Higgs boson seemed almost impossible. Hence, it was dubbed the 'God particle.' Both the Fermilab in the United States and CERN in Europe were in a race to find this elusive, theoretical particle. Eventually, in 2013, Peter Higgs and François Englert, who had theoretically proposed the Higgs boson, were awarded the Nobel Prize in Physics.

The Higgs boson could be a crucial key in opening up the closed system of science. It might be essentially a momentary energy (or momentary mass) created when a positron and an electron collide and are about to annihilate each other, then get trapped forever in the ice of time due to inflation. A singularity where gravity is so strong that not even light can escape is called a black hole. And a singularity where gravity is so weak that not even light can approach is called a white hole.

Within every Higgs boson, there might exist a white hole. Black holes and white holes are like two sides of the same coin. The event horizon of a black hole is the same as the event horizon of a white hole. If you look at the outside of a black hole from within its event horizon, it appears as a white hole. It's easier to understand if you think of it like a movie. The Higgs could be the boundary between a closed system and an open one.

Challenging the divine realm with science has always been considered forbidden territory. But with the Higgs boson, humanity sought to find a clue. Einstein opposed the probabilistic interpretation of quantum mechanics, stating, "God does not play dice with the universe." Steven Weinberg, a key figure in developing the Standard Model, said, "The idea that the laws of nature are somehow the expression of the mind of God is an overwhelmingly attractive idea." The reason this idea is so attractive is that science, having expanded its boundaries through human intellect and advanced civilization, has become the most significant threat to the absolute authority governing the world beyond our understanding. Perhaps this is the very frontier that an open system aims to reach.

Chapter 3

History of Open System

We believe that technology alone is insufficient.
This philosophy is embedded in Apple's DNA.
It is the fusion of technology and the humanities
that yields truly inspiring results.

- Steve Jobs

Beyond boundaries: Innovation through Openness

Open Sciences,
Open Humanities

Why must the humanities and sciences be separated?
Why does the gap between science
and the humanities persist?
To foster open science and open humanities,
efforts to bridge this divide are necessary.

An open-minded Western scholar who sought to learn about closed-off China

With the aspiration of becoming a well-educated engineer, I graduated from a chemical engineering department in Korea and began my career at the Korea Atomic Energy Research Institute.

In the 1970s, graduate programs in science and engineering were not as prevalent in Korea as they are today, so those aspiring for a Ph.D. typically had to study abroad in advanced countries. Back then, institutions like the Korea Atomic Energy Research Institute (KAERI) and the Korea Institute of Science and Technology (KIST) served as preparatory grounds for young graduates who dreamed of pursuing advanced studies overseas.

Caught up in this trend, I was preparing to study in the U.S. when I was selected for a government-funded scholarship and had the opportunity to pursue my studies abroad.

I specialized in fluid thermodynamics, a relatively scientific branch of chemical engineering. However, the engineering field I was in was rather niche and closed off. I began to ponder how I could make this complex subject more accessible to undergraduate students and the general public. That's when I conceived the idea of an "open system." While "open system" is a term from thermodynamics, it's also a concept that can be easily applied to the human world. As mentioned earlier, I decided to write this

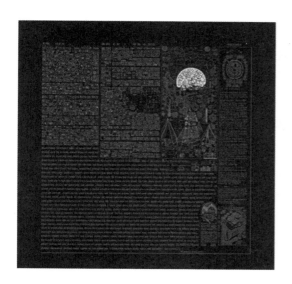

book with the goal of using "open systems" as a bridge to introduce the often secluded worlds of engineering and science to a wider audience.

Let's consider the readers as students and pose a practical question. Instead of asking a broad question like 'What is science?', let's ask a very practical one. Imagine you're aspiring to be a great scientist and you're given the opportunity to study abroad in a Western developed country. Given this chance, would you choose to pursue a graduate degree in your home country, or would you go abroad? Where would you ultimately decide to complete your graduate education? Domestically or abroad?

Of course, the quality of graduate programs in Korea has improved significantly over the years, and many programs are now on par with the best in the world. We no longer live in an era where studying abroad is a mandatory requirement. However, based on my personal observations, I believe that many of you would still choose to study abroad. Historically, for over 300 years, the education and research in science and engineering have been led by Europe and the United States. The Western world is considered the birthplace and symbol of modern science.

The leadership in modern science and technology is not proportional to the size of a country. There's no reason why a small Asian country like Korea can't become a leader in science and technology. However, as a Korean living in a country that isn't yet a leading nation in science and technology, I find the current reality quite bitter, but we have to accept it.

It is often said that the paths to science and engineering today all lead to Europe and the United States. However, this is not the whole story. If we look back in history, we find a time when all roads of science led to China and the East. There was a long period when the East was the center of human science and technology, and there are many scholars, both Eastern and Western, who study this period. A prominent example is the English biochemist Joseph Needham.

Before the 16th century, when Western science and technology surpassed the East, China was undoubtedly the leader in science and technology. China was so advanced that it captivated a Western scientist like Needham for his entire life, leading him to conduct extensive and meticulous research on Chinese science and civilization. What kind of country was China in his eyes? How brilliant was the scientific civilization of China, which was considered the center of the East from a Western perspective? How powerful was it? With an open mind, we aim to examine the level of science and the mysterious technological civilization of 'closed' China as seen through the eyes of the Western scientist Needham.

Until the 15th century, Chinese science was at a level that the West couldn't catch up to

While studying at Cambridge University and serving as a young professor there, Needham[3] was astonished by the scientific knowledge displayed by the Chinese students who came to study at the university. Through intellectual exchanges with these Chinese students, Needham was introduced to the splendid tradition of Chinese science and technology that had flourished from ancient times until around the 16th century. It suddenly occurred to Needham why China, with its superior scientific and cultural traditions, had not contributed significantly to the growth of human science and technology from the late 16th century onwards and had instead yielded the leadership to the West.

While the West, centered around England and France, made significant advancements in modern science and technology around the 16th century, why was China unable to continue developing its

---

3. Joseph Needham, a British biochemist and historian of science, began publishing his monumental work, Science and Civilisation in China, in 1954. This project continued until his death in 1995 and is still ongoing. Planned as a 7-volume, 34-book series, 19 volumes have been published so far. The general structure includes: Volume 1 (1 book) Introduction and background, Volume 2 (1 book) History of scientific thought, Volume 3 (1 book) Mathematics and the sciences of the heavens and the earth, Volume 4 (3 books) Physics and physical technology, Volume 5 (14 books) Chemistry and chemical technology, Volume 6 (10 books) Biology and biological technology, and Volume 7 (4 books) Social background.

science and technology and was instead stuck in place?

Needham dedicated his entire life to writing the monumental series Science and Civilisation in China to uncover the reasons why Chinese science and technology became stagnant. Beginning publication in 1954, Science and Civilisation in China emphasizes that the roots of science are not solely found in Western history but also existed in Eastern China. Initially, Needham wrote the book alone with the help of a few Chinese scholars. Later, it transitioned into a collaborative effort with various experts in specific fields taking charge of their respective areas.

Currently, a large-scale Needham Research Institute has been established in the UK, where the writing project continues. The vast Science and Civilisation in China clearly presents the achievements of traditional Chinese science and technology. Through this work, the previously little-known aspects of Chinese science and technology were introduced to a world dominated by Western perspectives. It is true that China's scientific knowledge and technological level were far more abundant and advanced than Europe's before the Renaissance.

According to Needham, from the 3rd to the 13th century, China created a level of science and technology far beyond anything the West could imagine. The various inventions, discoveries, and overall level of Chinese science and technology greatly surpassed that of contemporary Europe, with the gap being particularly significant before the 15th century.

[J. Needham, *Science and Civilisation in China, Volume 1 (Introductory Orientations)*]

Furthermore, from this perspective of the history of science and technology, it suggests that other civilizations besides the Western civilization of the same period also possessed a considerable level of science and technology. Moreover, this book provides evidence that modern science, born in Europe, owes much to Chinese science, prompting us to reconsider the nature of science and technology and the nature of modern science and technology. In other words, as evident in Needham's famous analogy that "the ancient and medieval science and technology of all nations and cultures are like rivers flowing into the ocean of modern science and technology," modern science and technology can be considered universal and global science and technology rather than 'European' or 'Western' science.

It can be said that Chinese science and technology made a fundamental contribution to the formation of modern global science and technology. Chinese science and technology also contributed significantly to the advancement of modern global science.

While Science and Civilisation in China achieved remarkable success in both the Western and Eastern cultural spheres, sparking significant reactions in the global scientific and academic communities, it also faced considerable criticism. For example, Needham categorized fields that played a crucial role in Chinese society, such as astronomy (tianwen) and geomancy (feng shui), which would fall under the 'sciences of heaven and earth' in Volume 3, as 'pseudo-science' and seemed to have neglected a proper examination of them. This highly ahistorical perspective has been a major obstacle to understanding Chinese science history within the context of Chinese history.

However, Science and Civilisation in China has served as a significant stimulus for scholars studying the history of science and technology in China and other East Asian regions with long cultural traditions. Moreover, this book has been both a valuable guide and a formidable challenge for them[4].

---

4. Kim Woo-chang, "103 Modern Thoughts," Minumsa, 2003.

■ China, One of the Birthplaces of Ancient Human Civilization[5]

China is one of the birthplaces of ancient natural philosophy, along with Babylonia, Egypt, and India

1. According to artifacts unearthed in Anyang, Henan Province during the Shang Dynasty in the 15th century BC, records indicate that the Chinese had already developed and utilized technologies such as bronzeware, chariots, silk, and rice cultivation. Furthermore, they are believed to have invented the sexagesimal system, a foundational concept in Western mathematics, possibly influenced by the earlier Babylonian civilization.

2. In the 6th century BC, iron technology developed in the Qin state, located in the western region. This technological advancement subsequently provided the foundation for the Qin Dynasty's military unification of China in the 2nd century BC."

3. During the Han Dynasty, which succeeded the Qin Dynasty, universities were established, learning was revered, and the

---

5. This is content that has been reorganized by traversing Google and Wikipedia.

early forms of bureaucracy were developed and implemented.

1) In the 1st century BC, the principle of the compass was invented.

2) In 105 AD, Cai Lun invented paper, and advanced technologies such as horizontal bellows, pulleys, belts, and vertical wheels for pounding grain were developed, marking a flourishing period for ancient Chinese science and technology."

4. In 480 BC, during the Qin and Han Dynasties, the philosophical foundation for natural philosophy developed.

1) During the Warring States period, one of the Hundred Schools of Thought, the Mohists, as a result of their research into preventing destructive wars, invented and utilized military training, optics, mechanics, and fortification techniques.

2) They invented and used the principle of light reflection using concave and convex mirrors, as well as the law governing the relationship between a mirror's curvature and the size and position of its image.

5. The Nine Chapters on the Mathematical Art was first compiled around the 10th century BC and was revised around the 2nd century AD. A glossary for the Nine Chapters on the Mathematical Art was created, and according to legend, it was said to have been made by the Yellow Emperor upon

the request of Jesus. This is the oldest collection of nine mathematical methods in China.

1) They invented the solving of simultaneous equations, the calculation of triangle areas, calculations involving positive and negative numbers, pi (π), and the square root of 10. However, it is unfortunate that there are no remaining records of using this geometry to quantify astronomical observations or to interpret the spatial structure of the universe.

2) Due to the algebraic nature of astronomical calculations, various cosmological theories emerged as they studied the structure of the universe. (For example, the Huntian theory.)

3) Unfortunately, they considered scientific experiments to be lowly, neglecting practical research that combined theory and experiment.

6. Song Dynasty: A large number of mathematicians, astronomers, and surveyors emerged. In Shu Shu Jiu Zhang (written by Qin Jiushao), advanced mathematics such as methods for determining the number of digits, the introduction of the zero symbol, algebraic methods for trigonometric problems, and high-order numerical equations and indeterminate equations were developed

7. Tang Dynasty: Paper, the compass, porcelain-making technology, woodblock printing, and gunpowder were invented

8. Han Dynasty: The development of papermaking led to the publication of many books. This technology was subsequently transmitted to Baghdad and, through the Crusades, to Europe, where it laid the foundation for Gutenberg's printing press.

Chinese astronomy,
which developed from philosophy,
was open system

When we think of natural philosophy or natural philosophers, we often immediately think of the early materialist philosophers of ancient Greece. Thales, Pythagoras, Heraclitus, and Empedocles are well-known examples of ancient Western natural philosophers.

In China, natural science and philosophy developed from the Spring and Autumn and Warring States periods. Confucianism, Taoism, and Mohism, which you've likely heard of, can be considered part of this group of natural philosophers.

Confucian thinkers were relatively indifferent to nature itself. Instead of focusing on nature, they tried to explain phenomena based on human ren (benevolence). Taoist thinkers, unlike Confucian thinkers, showed a deep interest in and curiosity about nature. They considered humans to be a part of nature and tried to observe nature more objectively. Therefore, they were critical of the human-centered thinking of Confucian thinkers. They placed great importance on logical thinking in science. This logical thinking became the foundation for optics, geometry, and mechanics. Gongsun Long(公孫龍) and Hui Shi(惠施) also emphasized the importance of logical thinking.

Thus, ancient Chinese natural philosophy developed significantly during the Spring and Autumn and Warring States periods (春秋戰國

時代). The Yin-Yang and Five Elements theory (陰陽五行說), a form of Eastern astronomy, also emerged during this time. Although there are countless claims and historical records about the Yin-Yang and Five Elements theory, in brief, it posits that the movement and development of the material world are the result of the opposition and harmony of the two attributes of Yin and Yang. According to the theory of the Five Elements, wood, fire, earth, metal, and water are considered the fundamental elements that make up all things. Furthermore, the theory posits that the mutual generation, overcoming, and restraint relationships among these elements are the fundamental principles of material movement.

This Yin-Yang and Five Elements theory developed into five forms of Yin and Yang. These are the five colors, the five grains, the five directions, the five musical notes, and the five human relationships. These five forms are considered the driving forces of history.

Especially noteworthy from the perspective of the development of ancient Chinese natural philosophy is that natural philosophers became interested in the universe and celestial bodies, and this developed into the Eastern form of the Yin-Yang and Five Elements theory(陰陽五行說). This was the beginning of an open system and an open discipline. We need to pay attention to this trend in Chinese astronomy, which evolved from philosophy to cosmic science.

Ancient China was home to several prominent cosmological theories, including the Gaitian (蓋天), Huntian (渾天), and Xianyaye (宣夜) theories.

The Gaitian theory posited that the heavens were like a rounded dome covering a flat Earth. The Huntian theory, on the other hand, envisioned the universe as an egg, with the celestial sphere resembling the eggshell and the Earth as the yolk.

From this period, ancient China began using a lunisolar calendar and developed theories to calculate the positions of the sun, moon, and planets, as well as to predict solar and lunar eclipses. This led to the emergence of astronomy, focused on observing the positions of stars.

The Xianyaye theory suggested that the universe was infinite, with the sun, moon, and stars moving along different paths within this vast expanse.

The development of these diverse cosmological theories stimulated a profound interest in celestial phenomena in ancient China. Astronomy evolved from mere observation to encompass celestial calculations, calendrical systems, and eventually, astrology. Moreover, the observation of celestial bodies and the associated concept of time led to the invention of sundials and water clocks, and the refinement of timekeeping techniques.

As China entered the Song (宋), Yuan (元), and Ming (明) dynasties, its astronomy built upon ancient cosmological theories and began to develop more sophisticated astronomical instruments. During the Song dynasty, the astronomer Su Song invented the Su Song Astronomical Clock Tower, a monumental astronomical instrument equipped with a mechanical clock, marking one of the earliest examples of mechanical clocks in human history.

By the Yuan dynasty, China began to adopt Western scientific knowledge. It introduced Western astronomy and constructed observatories like the Huihui Observatory. This period saw the introduction of advanced Greek astronomy, and Islamic astronomers were appointed as directors of these observatories.

China's Three Great Inventions overturned Western history

Francis Bacon, the 17th-century English philosopher, scientist, and statesman, credited China with three inventions that he believed had significantly contributed to the advancement of Western civilization: the compass, printing, and gunpowder. Bacon argued that these inventions were introduced to the West during the 14th century through the Mongol invasions.

This claim is widely supported by numerous historical accounts. Let's examine each invention in more detail: the compass, printing, and gunpowder.

First invented in China during the Han dynasty (3rd to 6th centuries AD), the compass was initially used for navigation. Its introduction to the West in the 13th century revolutionized maritime exploration, enabling longer voyages, increased trade, and the establishment of colonies. This played a pivotal role in the expansion of Western civilization.

The invention of movable type in China around 1040 and its associated printing techniques were introduced to the West in the 15th century, sparking the Printing Revolution. While this is commonly attributed to China, it's worth noting that Korea is also credited with developing metal movable type as early as the Silla dynasty, as evidenced by the Mugu Jeonggwang Dae Darani Sutra.

Originating in ancient China around 300 BC, gunpowder was introduced to the West in the 11th century. Its widespread use in Europe led to significant political and social changes, including the decline of feudalism and the rise of nation-states.

These three Chinese inventions have had a profound and lasting impact on world history. While the exact details of their transmission to the West may be debated, there is little doubt that they played a crucial role in shaping the modern world.

Ancient China was not only a birthplace of significant inventions but also a hub of diverse and innovative scientific discoveries. For instance, metal casting techniques dating back to 300 BC, including the use of temperature-controlled furnaces and molds, were introduced to the West around the 14th century, significantly contributing to Western technological advancements.

Moreover, the Chinese invented the seismograph in the 2nd century AD, demonstrating an early understanding of the Earth's spherical nature—a concept known as geocentrism. They were also able to calculate the number of continents and had developed concepts of latitude and longitude. These advancements were eventually transmitted to the West, leading to the widespread use of seismographs in geographical studies from around 1848.

Papermaking, another groundbreaking invention, originated in China around 200 BC. It spread to the Arab world by 800 AD. Europeans began importing paper from Arab lands in the 12th century and later developed their own papermaking industries.

Another fascinating invention from ancient China is the rocket. First developed during the Yuan Dynasty (13th century), rockets were initially used for fireworks and warfare. Multi-stage, long-range rockets were also developed. This technology was introduced to the West around 1380, significantly contributing to the advancement of Western military capabilities.

Lastly, it's worth noting a remarkable scientific discovery made in ancient China: the concept of inertia. Chinese philosophers, as early as 300-400 BC, had already articulated principles similar to Newton's Law of Inertia. The Mozi, a collection of philosophical texts, states that "a moving object comes to rest because there is a force opposing its motion." Mohist scholars made many other scientifically insightful observations that, unfortunately, are often lost to history due to incomplete records. It wasn't until the 18th century that the Law of Inertia was fully developed and codified in the West.

Sejong the Great, who embraced innovation by appointing Jang Yeong-sil, was a monarch with an open mind.

While Joseon's science and technology may have seemed modest in comparison to China's, they nevertheless made significant historical impacts, especially during the reign of King Sejong. Sejong's scientific endeavors were so advanced that they astounded both China and the rest of the world. Sejong embarked on a vast array of scientific projects, focusing particularly on astronomy and mechanics. These fields were closely intertwined with agriculture, as they were essential for determining the seasons and planning annual activities. As such, they became a royal responsibility, a way for the king to bestow 'grace' upon his people.

To foster scientific advancement, Sejong made a groundbreaking decision: he appointed Jang Yeong-sil, a former slave, to a high-ranking position. This unconventional choice shattered societal norms and exemplifies Sejong's open-mindedness. Despite being a slave, Jang Yeong-sil's exceptional talent as an inventor caught Sejong's attention. Sejong was a pragmatist who valued ability over social status.

Jang Yeong-sil hailed from the Asan clan. Born to a son of a gisaeng (a Korean courtesan), he was a slave in Dongnae County, Gyeongsang Province. Due to his humble origins, his exact birth date is unknown. However, he was said to possess an exceptionally

sharp mind from a young age. Known for his keen observation and mechanical aptitude, he excelled at creating, repairing, and modifying various devices. His skills also extended to metalwork, such as crafting and repairing weapons and agricultural tools.

Recognizing his extraordinary talent, Jang Yeong-sil gained recognition in his local community and eventually came to the attention of the royal court. It was during the reign of King Taejong, Sejong the Great's father, that Jang Yeong-sil was first recruited to work in the palace. However, it was under Sejong that Jang Yeong-sil truly rose to prominence.

Sejong, keen on advancing scientific endeavors, particularly in astronomy, sought to utilize Jang Yeong-sil's skills in metalworking, engineering, and problem-solving. However, appointing a slave to a high-ranking position in the royal court was unprecedented and faced staunch opposition from the nobility. Despite the resistance,

Sejong was determined to harness Jang Yeong-sil's talent and successfully persuaded his officials to allow the appointment[6].

In 1421, Sejong sent Jang Yeong-sil, along with Yoon Sa-ung and Choi Cheon-gu, to China to study astronomical instruments. Upon his return in 1423, at the age of 34, Jang Yeong-sil was freed from slavery and appointed as a Byeoljwa (別座) of the Sanguiwon (尚衣院, Bureau of Royal Wardrobe), a position that placed him in charge of creating and maintaining royal garments and other objects. This appointment marked a significant turning point in Jang Yeong-sil's life, allowing him to contribute significantly to the scientific advancements of the Joseon dynasty.

Under King Sejong's command, Jang Yeong-sil participated in a project to create astronomical instruments from 1432 to 1438, led by Yi Cheon. During this period, he gained immense royal favor by developing the Jaegakru (or Borugakru), a water-powered, self-operating clock, in 1434, followed by the Okru (or Heumgyeonggakru) in 1438. The Okru (屋漏)was an intricate device that replicated the rising and setting of the sun, allowing for the measurement of time, seasons, and celestial movements. A new building, the Heumgyeonggak (欽敬閣), was constructed specifically to house this remarkable clock.

In recognition of his exceptional abilities, Jang Yeong-sil was promoted from the position of Byeoljwa (a fifth-rank official in the Sanguiwon, or Bureau of Royal Wardrobe) to the rank of Hogun (護軍, a fourth-rank military officer) in 1433. The same year, he embarked on the creation of the Honcheonui (渾天儀, armillary sphere), which was completed in 1434. The

6. Abstracted from the Wikipedia

Honcheonui, also known as Seon-gi-ok-hyeong (璇璣玉衡) or Honi (渾儀), was an astronomical instrument used to observe equatorial coordinates and measure the positions of celestial bodies.

Even today, the Honcheonui (armillary sphere) proudly graces the back of the 10,000 won bill. The reason why Sejong could lead Joseon to its greatest era of peace, characterized by culture and reason, was undoubtedly due to his love of talented individuals and his unique human resource management system. His system was radical and open-minded, challenging conventional wisdom. Sejong tirelessly sought out hidden talents and appointed individuals as capable as himself to the right positions, orchestrating a harmonious blend of their skills and ideas.

Representative figures of Sejong's open-minded personnel policy include his political rival, Chancellor Hwang Hui, General Choi Yun-deok who made significant contributions to the Northeast Project and the conquest of Tsushima Island, and the slave-born scientist Jang Yeong-sil. While Sejong was a skilled politician, he also had a tendency to find it difficult to refuse requests. Despite being the frequent target of impeachment by the Saganwon (司諫院) and Saheonbu (司憲府) due to numerous corruption scandals, Sejong protected Hwang Hui and continued to employ him.

Moreover, he appointed Choi Yun-deok, who came from a lowly family, and entrusted him with the Northeast Project and the conquest of Tsushima Island. This earned Choi the reputation of 'Left (左) Yun-deok, Right (右) Jong-seo.'

Sejong possessed a philosophy that not only transcended the constraints of the class system in terms of talent recruitment but also advocated for employing individuals with exceptional abilities, regardless of their shortcomings. Due to his great appreciation for talent, Sejong had a unique leadership style of providing full support to individuals whose abilities had been proven.

Prioritizing ability over political considerations or societal norms, Sejong's rational approach to talent recruitment serves as a model example of open-minded leadership. This approach was the driving force behind the successful implementation of numerous innovative projects during his reign.

Jesuits: An Open Bridge Between Eastern and Western Science and Technology

It is intriguing to note that the missionary activities of the Jesuit Society in Europe during the 16th and 17th centuries in China and the East inadvertently provided an opportunity for the convergence of Chinese and Western science and technology. While engaged in missionary work in China, Jesuit priests played a pivotal role in the exchange and dissemination of traditional knowledge, science, technology, and culture between China, the East, and the West.

The Jesuits introduced Western science, mathematics, astronomy, the Western calendar, hydraulics, and geology to China, stimulating scientific inquiry in the country. For instance, Jesuit priest Johann Schreck published a Chinese-language book on Western mechanical engineering, introducing it to the Chinese public in 1627. Moreover, Father Matteo Ricci, along with Sabatino de Ursis, introduced Euclidean geometry, hydraulics, methods for predicting solar and lunar eclipses, and the Western solar calendar system to China, even reforming the Chinese lunar calendar using these Western methods (1582).

Johann Adam Schall, a German Jesuit priest, served as an advisor to the Shunzhi Emperor of the Qing dynasty. He established a Western-style mathematics school in China, introduced astronomy, and developed a Chinese calendar. After the death of the Shunzhi

Emperor, Schall sent numerous Chinese historical documents to the Vatican Library in Rome. Around this time, Fathers Jean-Francois Gerbillon and Joachim Bouvet introduced Western medicine to China, successfully treating the Qing Emperor Kangxi's illness in 1694. The examples mentioned here represent only a fraction of the Western civilization and technology disseminated by hundreds of Jesuit priests who resided in China for many years over several centuries.

In addition to transmitting Western culture and science and technology to China, the Jesuits also actively and enthusiastically transported China's advanced knowledge, civilization, and science and technology, which surpassed that of the West at the time, to Europe. Father Ricci, in his book De Christiana Expeditione apud Sinas, introduced Confucius's philosophy in detail. Later, along with Father Michel Ruggieri, he translated Confucius's Four Books and Five Classics into French, introducing them to the West.

Over subsequent generations, Western Jesuit priests who had experienced China (such as Father Philippe Couplet and Father P. Intorcetta) comprehensively collected and analyzed Confucian thought. They compiled it into French and introduced it to the West (1687). Subsequently, numerous similar publications related to Confucius and Mencius were published and transmitted to the West, resulting in continuous attempts in the West to philosophically integrate Confucian and Catholic thought.

Father Joseph-Marie Amiot, while compiling a French-Chinese dictionary (1789), played a significant role in introducing the vast expanse of Chinese science and technology to the West. Amiot authored nearly 15 volumes on Chinese science and art (1771–1791), further contributing to Western understanding of China. Many other Jesuits followed suit, publishing similar works.

Jesuit priests, renowned for their expertise in cartography, spent extended periods in China, conducting extensive explorations and astronomical observations. They created detailed maps of China, including precise latitude and longitude coordinates.

The scholarly correspondence between Father Joachim Bouvet and the German mathematician and philosopher Gottfried Wilhelm Leibniz offers another valuable glimpse into the advanced state of ancient Chinese science and technology. Bouvet, skilled in astronomy and mathematics, was sent to China in 1687 at the request of the French Academy of Sciences. Additionally, he was commissioned by Louis XIV of France to observe Chinese celestial bodies and gather geographical and scientific data from various regions. Accompanied by six fellow Jesuits, Bouvet spent several years in China carrying out his missionary work and royal commission.

Upon arriving in Beijing in 1688, Bouvet resided in the Kangxi Emperor's palace, offering advice on governance and even writing a biography of the Emperor. Intrigued by the Chinese concept of the 64 hexagrams, Bouvet engaged in a scholarly correspondence with Leibniz, one of the leading mathematicians and philosophers of his time (1701).

Gottfried Wilhelm Leibniz, a German mathematician deeply immersed in dualistic theology and philosophy in the early 17th century, developed the binary system.

Father Joachim Bouvet, a Jesuit missionary in China, introduced the Chinese concept of the 64 hexagrams (from the I Ching) to Leibniz through their correspondence. Bouvet explained to Leibniz how the binary system was implied in the 64 hexagrams, which sought to interpret Christian dogma, Chinese classics, the Taiji (Supreme Ultimate), yin and yang, the eight trigrams, and natural phenomena.

Through this correspondence, Bouvet and Leibniz engaged in a prolonged exchange of letters comparing Chinese philosophy, including Confucianism, with Christian thought. As a result of his correspondence with Bouvet, Leibniz became acquainted with Chinese history and the principles of the I Ching, which he subsequently introduced to others.

In 1697, Leibniz presented a more systematic binary numeral system to the Paris Academy of Sciences.

Thus, the Jesuit missionaries who spent extended periods in China, engaging in missionary activities, played a crucial role in introducing Chinese science and civilization to the West. Thanks to the Jesuits, the exchange of scientific knowledge between China and the West was carried out comprehensively and systematically.

It is truly fascinating that while China's unique science and technology were transmitted to the West, the leadership in global science and technology gradually shifted from China to the West. Conversely, although Chinese envoys and scholars were sent to Western powers, Western civilization and technology failed to spread to China and the East. This asymmetry in East-West interactions allows us to gauge the importance of an open-minded attitude of individuals, nations, or civilizations in accepting other cultures.

The Western scientific revolution, which started later than China's, surpassed China through its open scientific revolution.

Until the 15th century BCE, the West was relatively backward in terms of science and technology compared to the East (China). However, as mentioned earlier, Westerners who exhibited an open-minded spirit of exploration actively and comprehensively adopted Chinese science and technology, which was far more advanced. Traditionally, China's vast territory created a self-contained world, reducing the need to actively seek knowledge about the world beyond its borders. In contrast, the West, composed of smaller, neighboring states, recognized the importance of an open attitude in exchanging cultures and learning from others.

As a result, Chinese science and technology, which had spread to the West by the 15th century, were expanded and developed by Western scientists. Consequently, the 'Scientific Revolution' and the 'Industrial Revolution' that began in the 16th and 17th centuries were primarily led by the West, not the East.

The scientific and industrial revolutions that spanned over 200 years from the 16th to the 18th centuries in the West were unprecedented in the history of human scientific and technological advancement. The modern scientific revolution in the West led to Western dominance in modern science and technology. Countless scientists and engineers contributed significantly to this scientific revolution. To aid the reader's understanding, albeit at the risk of oversimplification, we will mention a few key scientists: Copernicus, Galileo, Kepler, and Isaac Newton, who will be discussed later.

During the scientific revolution of the 16th to 18th centuries in the West, Copernicus proposed the heliocentric theory, which was subsequently proven true through Kepler's astronomical calculations and Galileo's astronomical observations. Galileo was the first in the West to draft a system of mechanics to describe the motion of objects, and this classical mechanics was later systematized by Newton. These new scientific and philosophical arguments completely refuted the Aristotelian physics and astronomy that had previously dominated Western scientific philosophy.

To summarize briefly, Copernicus gave birth to mathematical astronomy and optics. He presented his research findings to the world in his work, De Revolutionibus Orbium Coelestium. Galileo further advanced celestial physics, and the scientific certainty of his heliocentric theory came to dominate the era. As is well known, Galileo's heliocentric theory overturned the geocentric theory of the Catholic Church, a historic event.

To avoid execution in the Inquisition, Galileo reluctantly testified that the geocentric theory was correct and the heliocentric theory was scientifically wrong, but as he left the courtroom, he famously protested, "And yet it moves." Galileo also invented the telescope, developed a pulse counter, and proposed laws of motion, making him a key figure in the scientific revolution. Kepler is revered as the scholar who discovered the solar system and further systematized cosmic science. In his work, Mysterium Cosmographicum, Kepler synthesized his lifelong research in astronomy, mathematics, optics, and celestial physics. He was also deeply involved in theology and metascience, leaving behind the famous saying, "Science is non-religious, and religion is non-scientific.

It was not only the scientists mentioned earlier. During this period, Gilbert conducted scientific research on magnetism, Paracelsus advanced medical science, and Vesalius systematically developed human anatomy. Additionally, Harvey discovered the scientific principles of blood circulation in the human body, laying the foundation for physiology.

Furthermore, the use of microscopes to study the growth of organisms began, as did experimental research to verify theoretical chemistry. Simultaneously, Newton and Leibniz developed calculus, which became the foundation for modern scientific inquiry and interpretation. Thanks to these revolutionary advancements, the new goal of science in the West was to observe natural phenomena as they are and to discover the objective and scientific truth of these phenomena.

Newton, Turing, Nobel
- Open-system Leaders
Who Led the Western Scientific Revolution

It was not only the scientists mentioned earlier. During this period, Gilbert conducted scientific research on magnetism, Paracelsus advanced medical science, and Vesalius systematically developed human anatomy. Additionally, Harvey discovered the scientific principles of blood circulation in the human body, laying the foundation for physiology.

Furthermore, the use of microscopes to study the growth of organisms began, as did experimental research to verify theoretical chemistry. Simultaneously, Newton and Leibniz developed calculus, which became the foundation for modern scientific inquiry and

interpretation. Thanks to these revolutionary advancements, the new goal of science in the West was to observe natural phenomena as they are and to discover the objective and scientific truth of these phenomena.

Newton, in his Principia Mathematica, reported his lifelong research to the Royal Society of London. Subsequently, he founded optics, calculus, discovered gravity, and formulated dynamics and the law of universal gravitation, solidifying his status as a core figure in the Western Scientific Revolution. At that time, Newton was even revered in England as a 'new Moses' in human history.

Darwin, through experiments and observations of nature, was the first in human history to propose the origin of species, plant hybridization, the theory of evolution, natural selection, and materialistic atheism. Notably, his proposal of the theory of evolution, which contrasted with Christian creationism, marked a significant turning point in human history.

Russian scientist Mendeleev proposed the Periodic Table, a systematic classification of all chemical elements. Often, a person who is skilled in many areas is called a Renaissance man, and this term perfectly suits Mendeleev. Through the periodic table, the grammar of chemistry, he arranged all known chemical elements by atomic number and systematized the periodic changes in the properties of basic elements, making a groundbreaking contribution to the foundation of modern chemistry and industrial development.

Additionally, we must remember Tesla, the developer of electricity and wireless communication, who brought immense progress to human history. It would not be an exaggeration to say that Tesla developed nearly all devices that utilize electricity. He invented the radar, fluorescent lamp, the precursor to the helicopter, neon signs, speedometers, automobile ignition systems, radio-controlled boats, microwaves, electron microscopes, anti-gravity devices, and countless other inventions. Considering that his lifetime research notes amount to 60 8-ton trucks, there is no need to further elaborate on Tesla's contributions to human science.

With the invention of computers and their subsequent integration as a cornerstone of human civilization, it's impossible to overlook the pivotal contributions of Turing to the field of artificial intelligence. Often hailed as the 'father of computer science,' Turing was tragically overlooked and even dismissed during his time due to his ideas being too advanced for his contemporaries. He proposed cryptography, perfected the theory of artificial intelligence, and advocated for artificial life.

Additionally, he authored a revolutionary computer user manual and made significant contributions to a wide range of fields such as computer games and computer music. Another well-known scientist is Nobel. His invention of dynamite has had a profound impact on the advancement of human civilization. Nobel successfully developed a solid explosive that eliminated the handling hazards of liquid nitroglycerin. His invention continues to be used in various mining, tunneling, and civil engineering projects. Nobel's contribution to humanity is further exemplified by his establishment of the Nobel Prize, funded by his personal fortune.

During wartime, wounded soldiers were highly susceptible to

bacterial infections, leading to a significant number of deaths. The discovery of penicillin played a crucial role in liberating humanity from diseases. This antibiotic was invented by Alexander Fleming, a scientist from St. Mary's Hospital Medical School in London, in 1928. During World War II, the American pharmaceutical company Pfizer began mass-producing penicillin, and it has since become a cornerstone of treating bacterial infections.

Lastly, let's examine the 'success through failure' story of Post-it notes, a Teflon adhesive that was accidentally developed in the late 20th century. Spencer Silver, a young scientist at 3M, was developing a strong adhesive when he mistakenly created a weak Teflon adhesive that could both stick very well and easily peel off. Initially classified as a failure, this adhesive was transformed through chance and thought. Art Fry, a scientist in 3M's commercial adhesive division, used the Teflon adhesive to create Post-it notes.

After numerous experiments to create a product that could stick to any surface and be easily removed without damaging paper, it was commercialized. Post-it notes were later selected as one of the "Top 10 Greatest Products of the 20th Century" by the Associated Press.

It is worth noting that the scientific revolutions that have transformed the paradigm of human civilization and the scientists who spearheaded these revolutions have originated from the West, not the East. 1 Moreover, it is noteworthy that scientific revolutions were rare in countries with highly closed political systems, such as communist states in the West. Why is this? And why were there no such scientific revolutions in countries like China, Japan, and Korea, which are relatively more advanced in science and technology compared to other Asian countries?

Perhaps it is because the West values free thought, while the East has a more bureaucratic and closed nature.

■ 100 Greatest Scientific Events That Changed Human Civilization[7]

1. **Use of Fire / Paleolithic Era:** Humans discovered how to control fire, which was crucial for cooking, warmth, and protection.
2. **Discovery of Metals / Neolithic Era:** The discovery and use of metals like copper and bronze led to the development of tools and weapons, marking a significant advancement in human technology.
3. **Invention of the Wheel / Sumerians, around 3500 BC:** The wheel revolutionized transportation and trade, making it easier to move heavy loads and explore new territories.
4. **Beginning of Greek Natural Philosophy / 6th-7th century BC:** The ancient Greeks began to question the natural world and seek rational explanations for phenomena, laying the foundation for modern science.
5. **Proof of the Pythagorean Theorem / 6th century BC:** Pythagoras and his followers made significant contributions to mathematics, including the famous theorem that relates the sides of a right triangle.
6. **Ancient Atomic Theory / Democritus, 5th century BC:** Democritus proposed the idea that matter is composed of indivisible particles called atoms, a concept that was later refined and developed by modern scientists.

---

7. Lee Jung-im, 100 Greatest Scientific Events That Changed Human History, Hakminsa, 2011, pp. 16-377

7. **Hippocratic Medicine / 5th century BC**: Hippocrates, often considered the "father of medicine," developed a rational approach to healing and established ethical principles for medical practice.

8. **Aristotle's Natural Philosophy / 4th century BC:** Aristotle's extensive writings on a wide range of subjects, including physics, biology, and metaphysics, had a profound influence on Western thought for centuries.

9. **Euclid's Elements of Geometry / 4th century BC:** Euclid's work on geometry provided a systematic and logical framework for understanding space and shape.

10. **Invention of Paper / Cai Lun, 105 AD:** The invention of paper by the Chinese enabled the widespread dissemination of knowledge and ideas.

11. **Ptolemy's Almagest / 2nd century AD:** Ptolemy's influential work on astronomy presented a geocentric model of the universe that dominated scientific thought for over a thousand years.

12. **Discovery of the Number 0 / 5th century AD:** The concept of zero and its use in the decimal system were developed by Indian mathematicians, revolutionizing mathematics and calculations.

13. **Invention of the Compass / 11th century AD:** The magnetic compass enabled sailors to navigate more accurately, leading to increased exploration and trade.

14. **Emergence of Metal Type / 1232 AD:** The development of movable type for printing allowed for the mass production of books and other printed materials, greatly accelerating the spread of knowledge.

15. **Discovery of the New World / Columbus, 1492 AD:** Columbus's voyage to the Americas connected previously isolated continents and sparked a new era of exploration and colonization.

16. **Heliocentric Theory / Copernicus, 1543 AD:** Copernicus challenged the geocentric view of the universe by proposing that the Earth and other planets revolve around the Sun.

17. **New Anatomy / Vesalius, 1543 AD:** Vesalius's detailed studies of human anatomy revolutionized the field of medicine and corrected many long-held misconceptions.

18. **Gregorian Calendar / Pope Gregory XIII, 1582 AD:** The Gregorian calendar

reformed the Julian calendar and is now the most widely used civil calendar in the world.

19. **Invention of the Microscope / Janssen, 1590 AD:** The microscope opened up a new world of microscopic organisms and laid the foundation for the field of microbiology.

20. **Thermometer / Galileo, 1593 AD:** Galileo's invention of the thermometer allowed for the accurate measurement of temperature, leading to advances in physics and chemistry.

21. **Study of Magnetism / Gilbert, 1600 AD:** Gilbert's research on magnetism laid the groundwork for the development of the compass and other magnetic devices.

22. **Kepler's First and Second Laws / 1609:** Johannes Kepler formulated his first two laws of planetary motion, describing how planets orbit the Sun.

23. **Telescope Invention / Galileo, 1610:** Galileo Galilei improved the telescope and made groundbreaking astronomical observations, supporting the heliocentric theory.

24. **Theory of Blood Circulation / Harvey, 1628:** William Harvey described the circulatory system, explaining how blood circulates throughout the body.

25. **Dialogue Concerning the Two Chief World Systems / Galileo, 1632:** Galileo's book defended the Copernican system and challenged the geocentric view.

26. **Scientific Method / Bacon and Descartes, 1637:** Francis Bacon and René Descartes developed the scientific method, a systematic approach to scientific inquiry.

27. **Experiments on Vacuum and Atmospheric Pressure / Torricelli, 1643:** Evangelista Torricelli conducted experiments demonstrating the existence of a vacuum and atmospheric pressure.

28. **Pascal's Principle / 1653:** Blaise Pascal formulated a principle in fluid mechanics describing how pressure exerted on a fluid is transmitted throughout the fluid.

29. **Discovery of Cells / Hooke, 1665:** Robert Hooke used a microscope to observe and describe cells in cork tissue.

30. **Invention of Calculus / Newton, 1669:** Isaac Newton developed calculus, a powerful mathematical tool for understanding motion and change.

31. **Classical Mechanics / Newton, 1687:** Newton's laws of motion and law of universal gravitation formed the basis of classical mechanics, describing the motion of objects.

32. **Steam Engine / Newcomen, 1712:** Thomas Newcomen invented the atmospheric steam engine, which revolutionized industry and transportation.

33. **Biological Classification System / Linnaeus, 1735:** Carolus Linnaeus developed a system for classifying living organisms, providing a framework for understanding biodiversity.

34. **Spinning Jenny / Arkwright, 1768:** Richard Arkwright's spinning jenny greatly improved the efficiency of textile production.

35. **Discovery of Animal Electricity / Galvani, 1780:** Luigi Galvani discovered that electric currents could stimulate muscle contraction in animals.

36. **Coulomb's Law / 1785:** Charles-Augustin de Coulomb formulated a law describing the force between electric charges.

37. **Alchemy / Hellenistic Period, 18th Century:** While not considered a science, alchemy was an early precursor to chemistry and contributed to the development of experimental techniques.

38. **Chemical Revolution / Lavoisier, 1789:** Antoine Lavoisier's work on combustion and the conservation of mass laid the foundation for modern chemistry.

39. **Smallpox Vaccination / Jenner, 1796:** Edward Jenner developed the smallpox vaccine, a major breakthrough in public health.

40. **Invention of the Battery / Volta, 1800:** Alessandro Volta invented the first electric battery, a device that could produce a continuous electric current.

41. **Revolution in Land Transportation / Trevithick, 1803**: Richard Trevithick developed the first high-pressure steam locomotive, revolutionizing land transportation.

42. **Invention of the Electric Lamp / Davy, 1806:** Humphry Davy invented the first electric arc lamp, a precursor to modern electric lighting.

43. **Atomic Theory / Dalton, 1808:** John Dalton proposed the atomic theory, which

states that all matter is composed of tiny indivisible particles called atoms.

44. **Law of Combining Volumes / Gay-Lussac, 1808:** Joseph Gay-Lussac discovered the law of combining volumes, which describes the relationship between the volumes of gases involved in chemical reactions.

45. **Avogadro's Law / 1811:** Amedeo Avogadro proposed that equal volumes of gases at the same temperature and pressure contain the same number of molecules.

46. **Synthesis of Organic Compounds from Inorganic Substances / Wöhler, 1828:** Friedrich Wöhler synthesized urea, an organic compound, from inorganic substances, challenging the idea that organic compounds could only be produced by living organisms.

47. **Non-Euclidean Geometry / Lobachevsky, 1829:** Nikolai Lobachevsky developed non-Euclidean geometry, which challenged the long-held belief that Euclidean geometry was the only possible geometry.

48. **Principles of Geology / Lyell, 1830:** Charles Lyell's book outlined the principles of uniformitarianism, suggesting that geological processes have been uniform throughout Earth's history.

49. **Law of Electromagnetic Induction / Faraday, 1831:** Michael Faraday discovered the principle of electromagnetic induction, which led to the development of electric generators and motors.

50. **Invention of Photography / Daguerre, 1839:** Louis Daguerre developed the first practical photographic process.

51. **Law of Conservation of Energy / Mayer, 1842:** Julius Robert Mayer formulated the law of conservation of energy, stating that energy can be converted from one form to another but cannot be created or destroyed.

52. **Surgical Anesthesia / Warren, 1846:** William T.G. Morton demonstrated the use of ether as a surgical anesthetic, revolutionizing surgery.

53. **Concept of Absolute Zero / Kelvin, 1848:** William Thomson, Lord Kelvin, introduced the concept of absolute zero, the lowest possible temperature.

54. **Bessemer Process / Bessemer, 1855:** Henry Bessemer developed a process for converting iron into steel, which greatly improved the production of steel.

55. **Theory of Evolution / Darwin, 1859:** Charles Darwin's book On the Origin of Species introduced the theory of evolution by natural selection.

56. **Refrigeration / Harrison, 1859:** William Harrison developed a practical refrigeration system.

57. **Internal Combustion Engine / Lenoir, 1860:** Étienne Lenoir invented one of the first practical internal combustion engines.

58. **Maxwell's Equations / Maxwell, 1864:** James Clerk Maxwell formulated a set of equations that unified electricity, magnetism, and optics.

59. **Mendelian Genetics / Mendel, 1865:** Gregor Mendel's experiments with pea plants revealed the basic principles of heredity.

60. **Second Law of Thermodynamics and Entropy / Clausius, 1865:** Rudolf Clausius formulated the second law of thermodynamics and introduced the concept of entropy.

61. **Dynamite / Nobel, 1866:** Alfred Nobel invented dynamite, a powerful explosive with many industrial applications.

62. **Transatlantic Telegraph Cable / 1866:** The first successful transatlantic telegraph cable was laid, enabling rapid communication between Europe and North America.

63. **Reinforced Concrete / Monier, 1867:** Joseph Monier developed reinforced concrete, a strong and versatile building material.

64. **Periodic Table / Mendeleev, 1869:** Dmitri Mendeleev created the periodic table, organizing the elements based on their properties.

65. **Telephone / Bell, 1876:** Alexander Graham Bell invented the telephone, revolutionizing communication.

66. **Germ Theory of Disease / Pasteur, 1878:** Louis Pasteur established the germ theory of disease, which states that microorganisms cause infectious diseases.

67. **Large-Scale Electric Power Generation / Edison, 1882:** Thomas Edison developed a practical system for generating and distributing electricity.

68. **Automobile / Daimler and Benz, 1885:** Karl Benz and Gottlieb Daimler independently developed the first practical internal combustion engines for automobiles.

69. **Electromagnetic Waves / Hertz, 1888:** Heinrich Hertz experimentally confirmed the existence of electromagnetic waves predicted by Maxwell's equations.

70. **Cinema / Lumière Brothers, 1895:** The Lumière brothers developed the cinematograph, a device for recording and projecting moving images.

71. **X-rays / Röntgen, 1895:** Wilhelm Röntgen discovered X-rays, a form of electromagnetic radiation that can penetrate many materials.

72. **Radioactivity / Becquerel, 1896:** Henri Becquerel discovered radioactivity, a property of certain elements to spontaneously emit radiation.

73. **Wireless Telegraphy / Marconi, 1897:** Guglielmo Marconi developed the first practical wireless telegraph system.

74. **Electron / Thomson, 1897:** J.J. Thomson discovered the electron, a fundamental particle of matter.

75. **Quantum Theory / Planck, 1900:** Max Planck introduced the quantum theory, proposing that energy is emitted and absorbed in discrete packets called quanta.

76. **Psychoanalysis / Freud, 1900:** Sigmund Freud developed psychoanalysis, a method for treating mental disorders.

77. **Blood Types / Landsteiner, 1901:** Karl Landsteiner discovered the ABO blood group system.

78. **Airplane / Wright Brothers, 1903:** The Wright brothers made the first controlled, sustained flight of a heavier-than-air machine.

79. **Vacuum Tube / Fleming, 1904:** John Ambrose Fleming invented the vacuum tube, a fundamental component of early electronic devices.

80. **Theory of Relativity / Einstein, 1905:** Albert Einstein published his theory of special relativity, revolutionizing our understanding of space, time, and gravity.

81. **Plastics / Baekeland, 1905:** Leo Baekeland invented Bakelite, the first fully synthetic plastic.

82. **Superconductivity / Onnes, 1911:** Heike Kamerlingh Onnes discovered superconductivity, a phenomenon where certain materials lose all electrical resistance at low temperatures.

83. **Continental Drift / Wegener, 1912:** Alfred Wegener proposed the theory of continental drift, suggesting that the Earth's continents have moved over time.

84. **Fruit Fly Genetics / Morgan, 1915:** Thomas Hunt Morgan and his colleagues used fruit flies to study genetics, leading to important discoveries about heredity.

85. **Radio Broadcasting / Westinghouse KDKA, 1920:** Westinghouse KDKA became the first commercial radio station, marking the beginning of radio broadcasting.

86. **Quantum Mechanics / Heisenberg and Schrödinger, 1925-1926:** Werner Heisenberg and Erwin Schrödinger developed the mathematical framework of quantum mechanics, describing the behavior of matter at the atomic and subatomic level.

87. **Penicillin / Fleming, 1928:** Alexander Fleming discovered penicillin, the first antibiotic.

88. **Expanding Universe / Hubble, 1929:** Edwin Hubble discovered that galaxies are moving away from each other, indicating that the universe is expanding.

89. **Particle Accelerator / Cockcroft and Walton, 1932:** John Cockcroft and Ernest Walton built the first particle accelerator, a device used to study the structure of atoms.

90. **Regular Television Broadcasting / Goebbels, 1935:** Joseph Goebbels played a significant role in the development of regular television broadcasting in Nazi Germany.

91. **Nuclear Reactor / Fermi, 1942:** Enrico Fermi led the team that built the first nuclear reactor, demonstrating the controlled release of nuclear energy.

92. **First Atomic Bomb / Oppenheimer, 1945:** J. Robert Oppenheimer led the Manhattan Project, which developed the first atomic bombs.

93. **ENIAC Computer / Mauchly and Eckert, 1946:** John Mauchly and J. Presper Eckert developed the ENIAC, one of the first electronic general-purpose computers.

94. **Radiocarbon Dating / Libby, 1952:** Willard Libby developed radiocarbon dating, a method for determining the age of organic materials.

95. **DNA Structure / Watson and Crick, 1953:** James Watson and Francis Crick

determined the structure of DNA, the molecule that carries genetic information.

96. **Sputnik / 1957:** The Soviet Union launched Sputnik 1, the first artificial satellite to orbit Earth, marking the beginning of the Space Race.

97. **Moon Landing / Armstrong and Aldrin, 1969:** Neil Armstrong and Buzz Aldrin became the first humans to walk on the Moon.

98. **In Vitro Fertilization / Steptoe and Edwards, 1978:** Robert Edwards and Patrick Steptoe developed the technique of in vitro fertilization, leading to the birth of the first "test-tube baby."

99. **Internet / ARPA, 1983:** The Advanced Research Projects Agency Network (ARPANET) evolved into the internet, a global network of interconnected computers.

100. **Cloned Dolly the Sheep / Wilmut and Campbell, 1996:** Ian Wilmut and Keith Campbell cloned the first mammal, a sheep named Dolly, raising ethical questions about cloning technology.

■ What kind of dream materials have accompanied the history of human civilization?[8]

①. Iron, non-ferrous metals, plastic, ceramic

②. Nylon

③. Synthetic rubber

④. Transistor, semiconductor

⑤. Superconductor

⑥. Super element C (graphite, diamond, fullerene, graphene)

⑦. Various vaccines

---

8. This is a re-organized content, crossing Google and Wikipedia.

The closure and openness of Eastern and Western science

Modern human society is still dominated by Western science and technology. In some ways, the gap between the West and other regions is widening to the point where it seems impossible for latecomers to catch up. The material culture achieved through modern scientific thought and technological innovation has become an absolute standard by which the world is viewed. As a scientist, it is truly disheartening to realize that science and technology have been used to support Westerners' sense of superiority over non-Westerners and their colonial policies, often justified by discourses of enlightenment, racism, and imperialism.

However, what is more important is the human-centered worldview that perceives human beings, who use science and technology to control nature, as superior to all other natural entities. The belief that all standards are human-centric objectifies and materializes everything else, reducing it to mere tools. This way of thinking, which has given rise to teleological and mechanistic views of nature, has led to terrible environmental pollution and alienation.

The core of Western science is rooted in rationalism and reason, which view the world as a kind of machine composed of parts, explaining how these parts connect through simple mechanical necessity.

However, armed with this mechanistic view of nature, Western science may no longer be able to sustain its power. The problems with this kind of science are evident in the fact that Eastern science once yielded its place to Western science. Astronomy (astrology), alchemy, paper, and printing were all invented in China first.

Marx called these the "three great inventions that heralded the arrival of bourgeois society" (Marx, Machinery: Application of Science to the Natural Forces, 1861–1863), and Francis Bacon stated, "These three things have changed the whole face and state of things all over the world, and brought in new instruments of power, so that they have given occasion to all the other great inventions, which have followed."[9]

So why did China's once great science succumb to Western and other civilizations and fail to regain its former glory? Joseph

9. J. Needham, 'Science and Civilization in China, Volume 1 (Western Part)

Needham, a British biochemist who devoted his life to studying China, would undoubtedly have lamented the decline of Chinese science. Why did China, with its flourishing scientific civilization, fall behind the West? The question of why modern science did not originate in China is one of the key issues examined in Needham's monumental work, Science and Civilization in China.

The reason why Chinese science declined and had to yield its position to Western science seems similar to the reasons why modern East Asian science and technology have failed to develop. In other words, the Confucian tradition of respecting elders in Eastern societies—a social atmosphere that favors older scholars with little ability over young, talented ones—limits the freedom of thought among young scientists. The formation of modern Eastern societies was not based on scientific rationality and logic, but rather on a bureaucracy that served as the dominant ideology.

In a bureaucracy-centered society, scientific debates and intellectual discussions cannot flourish. The problem lies in the fact that the core of East Asia's modern social development is bureaucracy, not scientific rationalism.

In contrast, the framework of modern Western society, as a result of the Scientific Revolution and the Industrial Revolution from the 16th century onwards, has inevitably been built upon scientific rationality and logic. This is a fundamentally different foundation from that of modern East Asian society. Given this perspective, there is an urgent need to systematically understand the scientific foundations and traditions of Western society, but the reality has been otherwise. Westerners tend to be efficient and capable when conducting research based on their own chosen internal criteria, while Easterners seem to be efficient and capable when acquiring what others (tradition) have defined.

In a way, Easterners have been sensitive to the evaluations of others, and as a result, have received an education that is uncreative and lacks originality. It is truly regrettable and bleak that this educational tradition seems unlikely to be easily improved in our society. Compared to the West, which values a modern and creative attitude, the Eastern academic tradition, which focuses more on results than on the process, needs to be urgently reformed. Moreover, unlike Western societies where scientists have been respected for a long time, the humanistic, bureaucracy-centered societies of the East can be said to hinder modern social development.

How about adding a science subject to the Korean civil service exam?

The 21st century we live in is undeniably a knowledge-based society, and at the core of this foundation is science and technology. Even those who prioritize humanities and literary knowledge would not deny this. Science and technology are the key pillars that determine a nation's competitiveness, as they are crucial for measuring trade balance and economic growth. Advances in natural science, applied science, engineering, and production technology are the real driving forces behind industrial development and acceleration.

However, how has science and technology education and research fared in our society since liberation? We have failed to patiently foster the growth of scientists and engineers and have instead been mired in a short-term, research-result-oriented system. Research funding has become bureaucratic and inefficient, and there has been neglect in developing creative talent. The root cause lies in bureaucratic, uniform evaluations and a disregard for individual characteristics. The bureaucratic decision-making of politicians and education authorities has been backward.

The 21st century we live in is undeniably a knowledge-based society, and at the core of this foundation is science and technology. Even those who prioritize humanities and literary knowledge would not deny this. Science and technology are the key pillars that determine a nation's competitiveness, as they are crucial for measuring trade balance and economic growth. Advances in natural science, applied science, engineering, and production technology are the real driving forces behind industrial development and acceleration.

However, how has science and technology education and research fared in our society since liberation? We have failed to patiently foster the growth of scientists and engineers and have instead been mired in a short-term, research-result-oriented system. Research funding has become bureaucratic and inefficient, and there has been neglect in developing creative talent. The root cause lies in bureaucratic, uniform evaluations and a disregard for individual characteristics. The bureaucratic decision-making of politicians and education authorities has been backward.

Furthermore, astronomical resources are required for the advancement of science and technology. Universities cannot solely rely on tuition fees, which can be considered a burden on students, to fund the resources needed for science and technology education. Like Germany, it is essential to have a national consensus that basic funding for the advancement of science and technology is a national responsibility, and that the government should invest in it.

South Korea ranks sixth in the world in terms of research and development investment. However, most of this investment is absorbed by corporations, while funding for universities is very limited. As a result, despite the quantitative growth in recent years (total R&D investment, R&D budget growth rate, number of researchers, SCI-indexed papers, and international patent applications), the qualitative level of science and technology and international competitiveness have declined overall. Currently, South Korea has almost no original technologies at the world's highest level. Moreover, in a society dominated by bureaucracy, the social perception of scientists is still not very positive.

So what are the solutions to overcome this national crisis in science and technology? Among the many possible alternatives, a few are as follows. First, structural innovation is needed in the government's R&D support budget. For example, investment in industrial and economic applied research and development should be shifted to be led by the private sector. Now, our country's support for the research and development sector should aim at fundamental science and technology research related to original technologies, or Prime Mover research, and there is a need to reduce support for technology-chasing or Fast Follower research, which South Korea has been actively pursuing until recently.

The government's policies and civil servants have played a significant role in transforming our country into a technologically advanced nation through technology-chasing research support over the past half-century. However, as our citizens' level of education has risen and science and technology have become more integrated, the cycle of technological change and revolution has shortened, and the useful life of technology has become shorter.

As a result, the cycle of economic activities based on science and technology has accelerated, necessitating a reevaluation of the scientific and technological level of government officials. One possible approach would be to include a science and technology subject as a basic examination subject in various national civil service examinations, regardless of the field.

Can the humanities resolve the crisis in science and technology?

Looking at the crisis of science and technology in our society, we can first find the seeds of the crisis and partial solutions by examining the historical characteristics that have shaped our society and the current social system. However, more fundamentally, where can we find the crisis of science and technology in the development of our society? It is true that our science and technology started from the beginning and development of science and technology led by the West hundreds of years ago.

Then, how can we break away from the reality of being under the shadow of Western science and technology and find our own way out of the crisis of science and technology in our society?

As a scholar who majored in engineering and has spent his whole life researching with students in his field, I have pondered a lot about this reality of ours. What are the expertise of science and technology, and what are scientific logic and rationalism overlooking? Also, how should we deal with the negative aspects of science and technology that are continuously pointed out in the humanities and social sciences?

The scientific and technological ideology centered on reason and logic has dichotomized nature and humans for hundreds of years, attempting to explain the world's problems through causality. 1 Other areas that have been excluded or neglected from science's linear thinking have often been dismissed as superstition or mysticism that disrupt our society. This harmful influence still dominates various aspects of our sociocultural life under the guise of scientific rationalism, causing significant damage. Many humanities and social science scholars have been acutely aware of and pointed out these dangers.

For example, Carl Jung, in his autobiography, Memories, Dreams, Reflections, argued that scientific rationalism and a kind of scientific dogmatism claim to have logical answers to everything, and that this is precisely the disease of our time. Does this mean that we can exclude scientific rationalism and reason in the present era? No. We must pursue different principles to overcome the limitations of science and related technologies so that they can become spiritually independent. What is that principle?

I believe the answer can be found not in single-minded thinking, but in diverse thinking, and perhaps even in the humanities, which may seem useless. What is the humanities? It is the study of human beings and fundamental human problems, thought, and culture, including classics, literature, philosophy, history, religious studies, linguistics, music, and art.

Kim Yong-min, a co-author of 'Humanities Recommended for Teenagers,' defines humanities as follows: "Humanities lead us to more fundamental questions. They explain who we are, where we come from and where we are going, what goals we should pursue, how we should live with others, how we should communicate with others, and why we feel joy, sadness, anger, and pleasure. In short, humanities teach us what our lives are made of."[10]

Humanities address what science cannot fully explain using scientific logic alone, and they help us understand the problems of our lives. This is precisely what can solve the problems overlooked by science. However, despite such an essential nature of humanities, we need to question today's humanities.

Can today's humanities truly fill the gap left by scientific logic? And can the humanities solve the numerous side effects that our society has experienced due to the advancement of science and technology in this era? I think we should carefully examine the crisis of our science and technology from this perspective.

---

10. Co-authored by Kim Nam-si, Kim Yong-min, and others, 「Humanities Recommended to Teenagers」, Geuldam Publishing, 2014, p. 34

Humanities should stand upright in their own place.

Most readers will remember Steve Jobs, the Apple CEO who was hailed as one of the greatest humanists of this century. We might ask ourselves, "How did a philosophy major end up becoming the CEO of Apple?" or "Why did he emphasize the importance of the humanities?" By pondering these questions, we can continually reflect on why he was called a champion of the humanities.

In truth, the humanities, by themselves, cannot be directly applied in a practical sense. Perhaps self-help books are more useful for us. Nevertheless, we read, learn, and study the humanities.

The renowned critic, Kim Hyun, offers a clear understanding of the nature of literature as a humanities discipline when he says, "Literature does not oppress, but it makes us think about oppression. This is because the non-oppressive makes us feel the oppressive more acutely"[11].

For Kim Hyun, literature, which makes us feel the oppressive through the non-oppressive, may seem useless in reality, but that is precisely its paradoxical utility. "Literature cannot save a starving

---

11. Kim, Hyun. What Does Literature Suffer For? In The Status of Korean Literature/Sociology of Literature. Seoul: Munhakwa Jisungsa, 1991, p. 54.

beggar. However, literature makes the existence of that starving beggar a scandal, and thus clearly reveals the identity of the oppression that suppresses humans. It sharply denounces human self-deception"[12].

If we can consider literature as the humanities in a broad sense, then the humanities make us feel the necessity to reform a world that is sickened by the contradictions of science and technology. We can then infer that we can obtain some wisdom through the humanities to overcome the crisis of science and technology.

Does the humanities truly have the power to reform the crisis of science and technology? Nowadays, the term "humanities" is used in many places. It is used haphazardly in countless book titles and lecture titles. Children's humanities, parental humanities, advertising humanities, CEO's humanities, the humanities of money, the humanities of love, the humanities of peace, biblical humanities, digital humanities... It's often said that a fish cake doesn't have a fish in it. So, do these various 'humanities' actually contain humanities?

And can we truly call this era, overflowing with such diverse rhetoric about the humanities, a genuine age of the humanities? Let's think deeply about this once more. When we look at the countless crosses in the city, do we think of a world filled with the Holy Spirit? If we unashamedly talk about the humanities everywhere without tension or a critical spirit, shouldn't we be wary of the possibility that the humanities could also degenerate into a

---

12. Kim, Hyun. What Can Literature Do? Ibid., p. 53.

mere business strategy?

The attitude that everything can be encompassed by the humanities should be reconsidered. If everything is included within that category, then conversely, it might mean nothing at all. Our approach to the humanities requires restraint and a sense of balance. We need to re-examine the humanities. In order for science to rely on the humanities, the humanities must stand firmly in their own place. To achieve this, we should reconsider the inherent isolation of the humanities, which is fundamentally asymmetrical to science, as well as the role of the humanities in education.

We need to pay attention to the asymmetry between the two academic fields: while someone with a foundation in science can begin studying the humanities, a humanist without a scientific foundation cannot suddenly start studying natural sciences.

For the past few hundred years, the fundamental ideological center of Western society has been, unlike ours, the rationality and logic of science and technology. However, the ideological center that has shaped our contemporary society is not science and technology, but rather humanities, social sciences, and bureaucracy. It is from this point forward that scientific logic and rational reasoning should naturally permeate our entire society. Such an awakening is urgently needed to remodel the castles in the air that are prevalent throughout our society.

Humanities and science, the East and the West are between the Cowherd(牽牛) and the Weaver Girl(織女)

Today, the humanities are often perceived as being in contrast or even opposition to the dominant elements of modern society, such as science, technology, and management. I am concerned that people might misunderstand science as being the antithesis of the humanities. Currently, the humanities and natural sciences are separated and isolated from each other. While it's true that in the West, a separation between the humanities and science and technology has existed since the scientific revolution of the 17th century due to the specialization of modern science, the situation in our society is much more severe.

A portion of modern humanities developed in the West has become fixed in our society in a form where science has been excluded.

Historically speaking, the humanities in our society have largely adopted the traditional objects and themes from the periods when modern humanities took root (such as the European Renaissance, the Song Dynasty of China, the European Enlightenment, and the modernization period in Korea).

However, in the past few hundred years, during which science has been excluded from the humanities, our society's way of life has undergone tremendous changes due to the influence of science and technology. As science has driven the advancement of civilization and assumed a new and important position, science, technology, information, and management have become detached from humanistic reflection and exploration.

Let's examine a case from Western society where serious concerns were raised about the asymmetry between the humanities and science and technology. At a gathering of British scientists, C.P. Snow, a scientist and journalist, remarked, "Scientists who do not know who Shakespeare is or who do not know his plays properly are quite ignorant."

He also noted that many humanists are not ashamed to admit their ignorance of the second law of thermodynamics, a core principle of physical science. It seems as if an insurmountable Jordan River flows between the two academic fields of science and technology, which is based on mathematics, and the humanities.

Why did we begin to establish such asymmetrical and rigid boundaries between the humanities and science and engineering?

The crisis of science and the humanities is causing serious problems due to the prolonged isolation between the humanities, science, and other specialized knowledge.

Let's consider the legend of the Cowherd Star and the Weaver Girl, who are located in the Milky Way. The bridge of magpies that allows them to meet once a year on the seventh day of the seventh lunar month connects these two. In other words, we must now undertake the task of building that bridge. Perhaps we ourselves must become the magpies and crows.

Shouldn't we now taste the joyful tears of the reunion of science and the humanities, as if it were raining on the evening of the seventh day of the seventh lunar month?

In fact, in the past, regardless of East or West, science and the humanities were not separated by such thick walls as they are now.

Let's briefly examine how the humanities and natural sciences interacted in the Eastern tradition. Historically, most humanists sought to include science or technology within the broad scope of the humanities rather than excluding them as knowledge that was not part of the humanities' spirit. In the past traditions of both East and West, the pursuit of scientific knowledge was considered part of a broader and deeper humanistic pursuit.

Zhu Xi (朱熹 1130–1200), in his works such as Zhuzi Wenji (朱子文集) and Zhuzi Yulu (朱子語類), viewed the fields of natural philosophy (astronomy, calendrical science, music, geography, divination, and medicine) and humanities (law, criminal justice, taxation, military affairs, and officialdom) from a fundamentally integrated perspective.

While he placed heaven, earth, all things, and humanity as the basic subjects of humanistic study, he also emphasized the importance and necessity of natural science and natural philosophy. He sought to include the fields of natural science and technology within a broad humanistic framework, and as a result, significantly influenced the Confucian (儒家) thought of later generations.

Zhu Xi's philosophical framework had a profound influence on prominent Confucian scholars in Korea, such as Yi Hwang (李滉), Yi I (李珥), Kim Seokmun, Yi Ik, and Hong Dae-yong, leading to a greater emphasis on the importance of natural science in their Confucian thought.

Confucius' saying, 'A gentleman is not a utensil' (君子不器),

originated from the emphasis on not reducing natural science to mere instrumental utility. It also stemmed from the desire to include knowledge of natural science and technology within the realm of humanistic cultivation and scholarship.

Confucius argued that a Confucian scholar should not be a specialist in only one field of the humanities. Instead, they should be an intellectual with a broad range of knowledge, including the humanities, natural sciences, philosophy, and technology.

It is also worth noting that Zixia (子夏), a disciple of Confucius, emphasized the importance of science (agriculture, horticulture, medicine, divination, and technology) in his Xiaodoguan (小道觀).

Western society has never erected a wall of separation between the humanities and natural sciences as stark as the one we have in Korea today.

Ancient philosophers such as Plato and Aristotle, while seeking the place and meaning of humans within the universe, considered natural science the foundation of the humanities. They pursued a cosmological view based on Christianity.

This characteristic is clearly evident in the curriculum of medieval European universities around the 13th century. Due to this philosophical background, the humanities, natural sciences, and technology have never been as severely isolated in the modern West as they are now.

Medieval European universities had a curriculum that integrated the humanities, natural sciences, and philosophy. From the Middle Ages onward, the university curriculum in the West placed great importance on natural sciences (arithmetic, geometry, astronomy, and music) within the broader framework of philosophy.

The roots of the humanities, which have been inherited and developed in both the East and West up to the present day, lie in the humanist thought of the Renaissance. The humanities, which blossomed during the Renaissance, included natural science, and, as a result, rapid advancements in natural science became a driving force for social change in the West. This laid the groundwork for the scientific revolution in Europe.

In Europe, natural science evolved from a simple exploration of nature driven by an interest in humans to a natural science that dealt with nature and the universe itself. This new natural science emphasized practicality and empiricism. As a result, it became the cradle of the Industrial Revolution.

Medieval European universities had a curriculum that integrated the humanities, natural sciences, and philosophy. From the Middle Ages onward, the university curriculum in the West placed great importance on the natural sciences (arithmetic, geometry, astronomy, and music) within the broader framework of philosophy.

The roots of the humanities, which have been inherited and developed in both the East and West to this day, lie in the humanist thought of the Renaissance. The humanities, which blossomed during the Renaissance, included natural science, and, as a result, rapid advancements in natural science became a driving force for social change in the West. This laid the groundwork for the scientific revolution in Europe.

In Europe, natural science evolved from a simple exploration of nature driven by an interest in humans to a natural science that dealt with nature and the universe itself. This new natural science emphasized practicality and empiricism, ultimately becoming the cradle of the Industrial Revolution."

Korean literature scholar Hwang Jong-yeon, a professor at Dongguk University, argues that the intellectual and literary innovations achieved by Yi Kwang-su in the 1910s have the character of a 'scientific turn.' Notably, the core of this turn is biology, especially the theory of evolution.

Lee Jae-seon, a senior scholar in Korean literature, has discussed in detail the characteristics and lineage of Yi Kwang-su's theory of evolution in his book Yi Kwang-su's Intellectual Wanderings (Sogang University Press, 2010), focusing on its relationship with Ernst Haeckel.

It seems certain that Yi Kwang-su, a literary figure of the early 20th century, planned to develop his own discourse across biological evolution, social evolution, and literary evolution.

A humanities student doesn't need to know science?

Although there may be differences in degree from ancient times to the present, no other country, like Korea, so severely isolates the humanities and natural sciences in education from high school to university. This isolation has negative consequences for the entire society.

Perhaps the most significant reason why the separation and divergence between natural sciences and humanities have become so severe in Korea is the harmful practice of dividing students into humanities or science tracks from high school for university entrance preparation. In other words, high school students are forced to choose between studying the humanities (humanities, social sciences, politics, economics, etc.) and natural sciences (mathematics, physics, chemistry, biology, and related engineering) for their future.

The most serious problem in this case is that it is extremely rare for high school freshmen to know whether they have a clear aptitude for either the humanities or sciences. Moreover, it is difficult to accurately assess whether a student's actual aptitude is more suitable for the humanities or sciences, and there is no rational mechanism for making such a judgment.

Furthermore, many students may have aptitudes for both the humanities and sciences. Despite this, all students are forced to choose one of the two areas—humanities or sciences—which is an undeniable reality of high school education in Korea.

Once they choose one area, they are confined within that choice and live a life isolated from the opposite field until they graduate from high school. Choosing one side becomes a necessary process for becoming an adult.

It is impossible to find any specific history or rational basis for how Korean high school education came to be this way. Rather, it seems that this division was established in a rather arbitrary and impromptu manner, relying on the power dynamics of the political sphere, rather than being based on rationality.

In the 21st century, we are living in a world of interdisciplinary studies. In a world where disciplines are integrated, students who receive limited education in either the humanities or sciences are bound to have very limited usefulness.

Recently, some conscious scholars in our society have been raising their voices to criticize the division between humanities and sciences.

In a 'Humanities Concert' in 2014, Do Jeong-il, dean of Kyung Hee University's Humanitas College, and Choi Jae-cheon, a distinguished professor at Ewha Womans University's Eco-Science Department and director of the National Ecological Research Institute, jointly pointed out the crisis that the high school-level separation of humanities and sciences has brought to universities.

Lamenting the education of Korean universities, which have been reduced to 'vocational training schools' for employment, Professors Do and Choi argued, 'The artificial and arbitrary division between humanities and sciences is a flawed system that our society has created for convenience at some point. It may be that we divide things because no one can do everything alone in the pursuit of truth. However, the two sides, which are educated in isolation, must inevitably meet at some point. There may be differences in whether we approach everything comprehensively or 'conquer each part individually' and then combine them. The idea that 'humanities students don't need to know science and science students don't need to care about the humanities' is simply unthinkable. I wonder where there could be a more primitive way of thinking'[13].

I fully agree with the timely observations of these two scholars in the humanities and natural sciences. The asymmetrical division

---

13. Scholarly Dialogue: Do Jung-il and Choi Jae-cheon Discuss the Intersection of Humanities and Science," published in Chosunbiz on November 1, 2014.

of humanities and natural sciences, starting from high school, is a recurring problem in Korea's academic and scientific circles. This arbitrary division between humanities and sciences, which has existed for too long in our society, has resulted in an extremely rigid and exclusive attitude towards the other side, whether it be the humanities or sciences.

Therefore, the arbitrarily divided and chosen boundaries between humanities and sciences become a clear and solid barrier of isolation even after education. This problem is no exception in universities, where the division of the two disciplines is found in every aspect of student life, such as professors, students, books, exams, and extracurricular activities, shaping students' growth, identity, and personality.

As a result, even after graduating from university and becoming ordinary citizens, people continue to accept the university's division of humanities and sciences as natural, which is also a serious problem.

In Korea, there have been some attempts to improve the problems associated with the compartmentalized humanities/science education and its negative impacts on society after graduation. The 1993 College Scholastic Ability Test is an example.

In this test, which was implemented suddenly in 1993, all test-takers, regardless of their humanities or science focus, were required to solve the same problems as a pilot project. However, students accustomed to the segregated humanities/science education were unable to adapt to this change.

As a result, the public perceived this method as hindering the development of the relatively balanced humanities/science-specific 'College Scholastic Ability' that had existed before. Some scholars argued that 'since this test is not for measuring academic ability by field but for evaluating academic ability in university, it is a principle not to separate them'[14], but this opinion was not accepted.

This led to unfair advantages and disadvantages between humanities and science students in the exam. Instead of seeking a more balanced high school education, the education authorities introduced a new, separate humanities/science test system."

There exists a deeply ingrained custom among teachers, parents, educators, and politicians to rigidly adhere to the division between the humanities and sciences in all aspects of life, both academic and otherwise. Any attempt to challenge this division is met with staunch resistance.

The harms of dividing students into humanities and science tracks are severe. One of the most serious consequences is that the rigid boundary between these two tracks significantly narrows the scope of students' studies.

For instance, a student aspiring to study economics, classified as a humanities student, may neglect or ignore essential natural sciences such as mathematics and physics when entering university. Similarly, a business major, categorized as a humanities student for convenience, can enter university without any institutional encouragement to be interested in natural sciences or technology. Students aiming for computer science or oceanography may

14. November 17, 1993, Dong-A Ilbo, page 21, social news.

mistakenly believe that, as science students, they can ignore the humanities and social sciences during their exam preparation.

People immersed in this trend even take the initiative to label themselves as either humanities or science students, believing they have no need or ability to understand the other side. This misjudgment breeds ignorance of the other side and normalizes it. It's truly absurd that our education authorities and educators have been advocating for such a thing.

In the 21st century, human civilization has experienced rapid development. Societies and cultures in all countries are now becoming increasingly complex, giving rise to various interdisciplinary fields. Environmental science, information science, integrated software, agriculture, architecture, urban planning, and many others are areas where the humanities/science divide is inappropriate.

Additionally, countless new disciplines such as planning, physical education, psychology, geography, oceanography, and business management have emerged. However, our educational reality forces students into rigid categories and directs them towards a specific approach within each field. As a result, new interdisciplinary fields struggle to develop independently.

Isn't the time to start making changes precisely when we say it's too late? It's time to eliminate the humanities/science division and segregated education that begins in high school. Only then will our society have a future and hope. With such a meaningful foundation, open curriculum projects at universities will gain significant momentum.

Education that cannot nurture dreams is a closed education

While it's commonly believed that the concept of a 'university' originated in the West, institutions similar to universities did exist in ancient China and the Arab world. Nevertheless, the university system that has truly evolved and been inherited by human society is that of 13th-century medieval Europe.

For hundreds of years following, medieval European universities were traditionally composed of four faculties, a structure that persisted until the late 19th century. These four faculties were philosophy, theology, law, and medicine. Among these faculties, science was considered a foundational, liberal arts subject before the Scientific Revolution of the 16th and 17th centuries. The seven liberal arts included the quadrivium (arithmetic, geometry, astronomy, and music) and natural philosophy, a part of philosophy.

The perception of science in the West underwent a visible and positive transformation in general society after the Scientific Revolution of the 16th and 17th centuries. However, until the onset of this revolution, Western universities often acted as bastions of resistance rather than welcoming new scientific advancements.

Even in the West, universities often remained isolated from society, indifferent or even resistant to societal progress and development outside of academia. Thus, they alienated themselves from the civilizational evolution of the external world.

From its emergence in the 13th century until the Scientific Revolution of the 16th century, the Western university system remained entrenched in Christian theology and scholastic logic, with a heavy emphasis on textual analysis. As a result, universities were sometimes dismissed as places where one learned only useless things upon entering society.

This isolation from society led to the perception that universities were inherently resistant to change. Consequently, universities sometimes failed to respond promptly to societal changes. However, society grew increasingly dissatisfied with the exclusive knowledge monopoly held by universities and with the knowledge they provided in isolation.

The primary achievements and changes brought about by the 16th-century Scientific Revolution occurred not within the confines of universities but were driven primarily by academic societies outside of universities, such as the Royal Society of London and the French Academy of Sciences.

In the West, the Scientific Revolution led to the Industrial Revolution, making natural sciences and the natural philosophy based upon them fundamental frameworks for Western societal development, rivaling the humanities.

Indeed, the natural sciences and related technologies developed in Europe from the late 19th century onward became the model for global science and technology today. Universities, which had been isolated from society until the 19th century, were forced to embrace change rather than resist the demands for reform coming from outside their walls.

Germany, in particular, having suffered defeat in the Napoleonic Wars, took the lead in autonomously driving the wave of university reform among European powers.

Germany pioneered a shift away from the traditional, one-way lecture style, particularly in the sciences and technology. This shift was towards a more interactive seminar-based approach where professors and students could freely exchange academic ideas on equal footing.

This two-way educational method involved students actively researching and presenting their findings on the lecture topics, allowing for the sharing of knowledge not only from the professor but also from the students. Simultaneously, a strong emphasis was placed on experimental learning, complementing theoretical knowledge in the sciences and technology.

Initially adopted in the sciences and technology, this interactive and experimental approach was gradually extended to fields like history, literature, and philosophy. This pioneering educational reform in Germany was subsequently adopted by other Western countries as a new pedagogical model.

Furthermore, professors began to secure external funding for research projects and involved their students, doctoral candidates, and postdoctoral researchers in these projects. This ensured the rigor of research and provided students with valuable hands-on research experience.

Students received a modest stipend for their involvement, enhancing their financial stability during their studies. The knowledge and skills acquired through research participation also gave students a competitive edge in the job market. This tradition of fostering collaborative research was a testament to German ingenuity.

The practice of involving students in research, beyond simply attending lectures, gradually expanded from the sciences to the humanities and social sciences, including history, literature, and philosophy. This innovative teaching method was subsequently adopted by other Western countries.

What about the United States after the 19th century? The U.S. was also quick to adopt a research-oriented approach to higher education.

In the 19th century, many American universities (such as Johns Hopkins, and Ivy League schools like Harvard, Yale, UPenn, Columbia, Brown, Dartmouth, and Cornell) adopted the German model of two-way, research-focused education, particularly at the graduate level.

After the Civil War, the U.S. shifted its higher education focus from the traditional British model centered on classical languages, faith, and moral education to practical knowledge that better met the demands of modern society, such as modern languages, natural sciences, and technology.

This period saw unprecedented and rapid advancements in natural science and technology. As a result, interdisciplinary fields in American universities expanded significantly and became more specialized. Engineering education experienced a golden age focused on the practical application and industrialization of science and technology.

This led to a paradigm shift in higher education worldwide. It was during this period that the popular field of business administration emerged in American universities.

Turning to Japan, the Westernization process led to the establishment of European and American-style universities. 1 Imperial universities (such as Tokyo, Kyoto, Tohoku, Hokkaido, Kyushu, and Nagoya) transformed into Western-style research-focused institutions, serving as the foundation for Japan's national wealth.

Japan invested enormous resources and carefully prepared for the introduction of Western-style universities, successfully adapting these imported systems to fit their own context. Numerous documents attest to these efforts.

So how has the transplantation and development of Western-style universities been in South Korea? As mentioned earlier, due to the humanities/science division in high school, our university system is still rigidly divided into humanities, economics, and social sciences on one side, and engineering and management on the other. As a result, rigid walls have been erected between different colleges within the same comprehensive university.

Let's examine the issue of students' academic self-determination in universities.

For example, consider the situation of engineering students who have studied mathematics and natural sciences in high school, compared to humanities students who have not taken natural science courses and have directly entered university. While engineering students can take humanities courses if needed, humanities students, lacking the foundational knowledge of mathematics and natural sciences, cannot study natural sciences or engineering. This creates a severe imbalance between disciplines.

Consequently, once students enter a university and choose their major, all academic decisions within the university are made within the framework of individual colleges or departments. This leads to a fixed, asymmetrical barrier of communication between disciplines, solidifying the rigid distinction between humanities/science, and the humanities, social sciences, natural sciences, and technology.

This arbitrary and convenient division of academic courses within universities fundamentally prevents graduates from understanding the complex developments of modern society and the cultural phenomena intertwined with natural science.

What about the social reality outside of universities? The pace of societal development and civilization is incredibly rapid. Recently, a new, integrative culture has emerged in our society, breaking down the asymmetrical equilibrium between the humanities and sciences. Society now demands university graduates who possess a comprehensive understanding that transcends the traditional humanities/science divide.

Simultaneously, university education is divided into two tracks: cultivating future generations of academics (general scholarship) and training professionals to meet immediate societal demands (specialized occupations). This division is reasonable. However, the problem lies in the current indiscriminate manner in which these human resources are being trained.

At this point, we must question whether humanities education in our universities is truly effective. Since modernization, the development and education of the humanities in our country have been influenced by modern China, although the extent of this influence is uncertain. There has been an excessive focus on cultivating humanities-based bureaucrats for the civil service. Rather than nurturing young people to become the kind of individuals society needs, humanities education has been primarily focused on the ruling class and the intellectual elite.

Following liberation, our country's modernization process naturally adopted the curricula of the United States and European countries, which were far more economically powerful than we were. As a result, we became disconnected from our historical traditions, and even humanities within universities became detached from pre-modern traditional scholarship.

As I will mention later, it's not as if our society has thoroughly benchmarked the Western university model. In a sense, we only adopted the superficial aspects, while neglecting the core issues such as tenure systems, competition and sustainability among academic disciplines, which became intertwined with our bureaucratic system. The consequences of this neglect persist in our universities today.

Have our humanities students truly contemplated the meaning of humanity before choosing their major? This is not a problem limited to humanities students alone.

Most students spend their entire high school years immersed in the inhumane process of preparing for college entrance exams. From the perspective of the privileged generation, it is inevitable to conclude that these young people are enduring a period of severe human rights violations where their self-determination is completely denied.

As a university president who has spent decades as a professor, I believe this is a matter that we must reflect upon.

We spend a significant portion of our high school education on studies that do not contribute to the free intellectual growth of young people. Instead, this education forces them to focus solely on producing the numbers needed for university entrance exams.

If, during the era of vibrant democratization movements in our country, not only young people but any social group had been forced to endure the suppression of education solely for college entrance and the deprivation of self-determination against their will, there would undoubtedly have been immense resistance and struggle. However, the current dominant generation, including myself, has merely imposed the assertion, 'Just endure it a little longer, and you'll succeed,' on young people, without providing any sound reasoning. We must seriously reflect on this failure.

We need to create an optimal environment through university and educational reforms where new generations can build hope and open up their futures. To achieve this, the older generation must take the first step in implementing change.

The crisis of humanities in Korea is as severe as the crisis in science

Fundamentally, regardless of East or West, the humanities today can trace their roots back to humanism, which originated from the Renaissance movement in the West.

In Western history, the influence of Christian faith was far more powerful than Confucianism or Buddhism in the East. The history of universities, which began in 13th-century Europe, was dominated by Christian-oriented disciplines such as theology, logic, metaphysics, and natural philosophy due to the influence of the Catholic faith.

However, as centuries passed, the corruption of Christianity led to the Renaissance as a movement to revive it. After the Renaissance, as a natural reaction against the theology-centered, Christian-focused scholarship, a humanistic paradigm emerged that shifted the focus to human beings.

The humanities sought to find new humanistic changes by rediscovering the ideas of ancient Greece and Rome that predated Christianity. As a result, the humanities after the Renaissance tended to respond to new social movements.

Subsequently, the humanities evolved from theological classical studies and classical languages to modern languages and practical studies. And Korea, having imported the Renaissance-style humanities from the West, continues to adopt its content today.

Amidst the widespread crisis of the humanities in our society, it is time for us to reflect on the true nature of this crisis and seek alternatives. In a way, our humanities today lack a thorough self-reflection, criticism, and the effort to propose progressive perspectives.

The crisis in our humanities stems from our neglect of the need to expand the foundation of humanistic knowledge as demanded by societal development. In a sense, the true crisis of the humanities, as it is referred to in our society, seems to reflect a series of survival tensions among humanities scholars, arising from their attachment to old frameworks.

In a situation where society is developing and moving away from universities, it seems that in order to avoid the crisis of the humanities, we are becoming even more attached to traditional humanities.

By examining the recent state of our society and universities, we can more clearly understand the true nature of the humanities crisis.

For instance, on September 15, 2006, all 121 professors of the College of Liberal Arts at Korea University called for the overcoming of the 'humanities crisis' on the 60th anniversary of the college's founding. This was a signal flare announcing the 'humanities crisis theory.'

On September 25, 2006, deans of 80 humanities colleges nationwide, ahead of the 'Humanities Week' opening at Ewha Women University on the 26th, issued a declaration titled 'Our Proposal for the Humanities Today,' arguing that the disregard for the humanities was the root of the crisis.

They proposed concrete measures to promote the humanities, such as universities not simply conforming to consumer demands or market logic, establishing a 'Korean Humanities Committee' (tentative name) to plan and implement long-term development strategies, establishing a 'Humanities Promotion Fund' for continuous support, and guaranteeing the participation of humanities scholars in major national policy committees.

Of course, these claims should be humbly accepted. However, it is worth considering whether such movements have genuinely taken into account the perspective of parents who send their children to study humanities in universities.

We must reflect on whether the current movement to revive the humanities in our society is merely a desperate attempt to defend traditional humanities in the face of a changing social reality where the space for the humanities is becoming increasingly narrow.

As we all know, there is a growing social demand for change in universities. While the economy is expanding, job opportunities for young graduates who have studied only traditional humanities are decreasing at an alarming rate. Humanities departments in universities are being prioritized for mergers or closures, and the employment rates of graduates are plummeting.

The humanities that society demands are not traditional humanities themselves, but rather academic changes that can be more deeply integrated into all practical disciplines. What is the true cause of the humanities crisis in universities?

It is wrong to simply condemn the tendency of companies and society to prioritize engineering or business majors in new employee selection as mere 'market logic.' The university graduates that companies need, regardless of their major, are those with a solid foundation in the humanities.

Therefore, we should not simply evaluate the humanities in universities based on the low employment rates of humanities majors. The humanities are now at opposite ends when it comes to post-graduation employment. It is true that humanities majors are currently facing neglect in terms of employment, but I believe that through this reality, the humanities will evolve and become more positive.

As industries become more advanced, there will be a growing recognition that the incorporation of humanities into natural science and engineering knowledge is essential for a positive corporate future. Opportunities will expand for young people with humanities-based skills when seeking employment.

For example, the 'POSCO Scholarship' is a pre-employment program designed to foster creative talent with the ability to integrate the humanities and sciences. Outstanding second-year university students are selected early and encouraged to take humanities courses in science majors and science courses in humanities majors during their studies[15].

Samsung's 'humanities and sciences convergence' talent development plan is similar. Samsung Group has recently finalized and announced a more advanced human resources policy to foster software engineers from humanities majors[16].

This change in corporate perception of new employee recruitment is clearly a positive sign for the evolution of the humanities in universities.

The humanities should now be considered not merely as traditional humanistic knowledge, subjects, or fields of study, but rather as humanistic methods or spirits that should be widely contemplated across diverse academic disciplines.

Furthermore, the humanities should no longer be confined to a specific part or class of our sociocultural sphere but should permeate all of cultural society as a fundamental framework.

As new ideas and cultures give rise to new values and problems, demanding a transformed humanities, this may very well be a groundbreaking turning point for the development of the

---

15. Maeil Business Newspaper, Korea, October 29, 2013

16. Munhwa Ilbo, Korea, March 13, 2015, page 1.

humanities. We anticipate a proactive movement to transform the humanities into a discipline that deals with new knowledge, subjects, and objects, as new social and cultural phenomena are included within its purview.

Both humanities scholars and natural scientists are closed systems if they lack imagination

The crisis is not limited to the humanities alone. We must keenly recognize that natural sciences, engineering, and other practical disciplines are also facing a crisis.

Both in Korea and globally, as modern society becomes increasingly scientific, technological, and informational, we are suffering from numerous negative consequences related to natural science, technology, and information.

For humans, natural science is undoubtedly a tool of civilization. In particular, the progress of natural science in this century has accelerated the development of civilization. However, this scientific and technological, as well as information-oriented world, does not always bring happiness to humanity.

The self-interest of natural science is passed on to humans, preventing us from thinking about what it means to be human and how we should behave.

While the humanities may not provide definitive answers to the age-old question of what it means to be human, they encourage us to constantly ponder this question.

The reflective thinking of the humanities should be expanded with the advancement of science. The critical thinking and rich imagination of the humanities should stimulate the progress of natural science, and the technological imagination of natural science should stimulate the critical imagination of the humanities.

To achieve this, both the humanities and natural sciences must actively open their doors to each other and communicate.

Let's recall the anecdote of Isaac Newton observing an apple falling from a tree in his mother's garden. Even if Newton had thrown the apple, it would have flown forward in a parabolic trajectory for a certain distance before eventually falling to the ground.

'Why does the apple fall?' Newton wondered. 'What if I threw the apple harder?' It would fly farther, but eventually, the apple would still fall to the ground. The reason we can make such an assumption is that we now know that the Earth's own gravitational force pulled the horizontally flying apple back down to the ground.

While there may be no readers today who are making the same assumptions and asking the same questions as Newton, the 'imagination of a falling apple in flight' that Newton engaged in is significant. If Newton had not pondered why the apple fell to the ground, we might still believe that the Earth's gravitational world and the celestial world are separate, and we might not have been able to create countless satellites that orbit the Earth in a zero-gravity space as we do today.

Regardless of East or West, the rise of modern realism and naturalism was significantly influenced by the changing cognitive system and methodology of modern science. Writers who adopted the scientific method of objectively observing and analyzing reality from natural science also sought to cultivate a method of objectively observing and narrating human social reality.

From this perspective, we can nod in agreement with Louis Mink's assertion that 'narrative' is a 'fundamental cognitive tool of history,' comparable to a scientific theory or a literary metaphor. Narrative is a form that allows us to understand the sequential interrelationships of a series of events or phenomena contained within it.

Narrative, which allows us to understand the flow of experience, can be a fundamental cognitive tool of history.

Today's universities, particularly in the realm of natural sciences, should go beyond teaching students their specialized fields and also cultivate their humanistic imagination. Whether majoring in the humanities or natural sciences, students should be able to cultivate 'imagination.' This imagination is neither exclusive to the humanities nor to the natural sciences, but rather serves as a bridge connecting the two.

Evolutionary biologist Jang Dae-in, in his book What Science Tells Us About Humans, divides humans into 'Homo Scientificus' (the exploring human), 'Homo Replicus' (the imitating human), 'Homo Empathicus' (the empathetic human), 'Homo Religious' (the believing human), and 'Homo Convergenicus' (the converging human)[17].

Today's universities need to focus on educating individuals who can integrate and converge different academic disciplines. Contemporary universities must move away from the uniform and standardized traditional education.

---

17. Jang Dae-ik, What Science Tells Us About Humans, Bada Publishing, 2013.

The future society demands a mutually complementary relationship between the humanities and natural sciences. Even in university lectures, the two cultures must be able to communicate, and such opportunities must be created.

Universities must evolve by breaking away from traditional and conservative attitudes and adapting to the demands of the times and the future. I hope that universities will move towards a path where the two fields meet, in line with the goal of 'convergence' for future universities.

In this era of transition, what is the responsibility of the state? The government must completely abandon the notion of viewing universities as objects of control. The reality in Korea, where the government imposes excessive regulations and controls on universities, is unprecedented in any advanced country.

To exaggerate a bit, it seems like our country's education authorities are imposing nearly socialist-level regulations and strict controls. This is because they are taking the initiative to lead university reforms by wielding clumsy 'carrots and sticks' over almost all aspects of universities, including enrollment, tuition fees, and graduate schools. As a result, each university seems to be taking on a uniform appearance, lacking its own unique characteristics or specialized programs. This is a time when serious reflection and consideration are needed.

Chapter 4

The Challenge of an Open System

Horizontal and open thinking is being 'ordered'.
An era has come where the horizontal thinking of
nomads who roamed the world without knowing
boundaries or walls is desperately needed.

- From Kim Jong-rae's CEO Genghis Khan

Beyond boundaries: Innovation through Openness

Knock!
And it will be opened to you

(Matthew 7:7)

Airbnb founder Joe Gebbia received cheers when he said,
'When people say, "Are you crazy?",
it's proof that you're doing something right.'
In our society, it's an era of managing both failure and challenge.
If people in their 20s, who haven't even taken their first step into society,
are giving up and falling down after just
a few failures, it's not only a personal misfortune but also
a national waste

The challenge of an open world, a world of open challenges

As a member of the post-war generation, I entered university in 1970. At that time, both the country and the people were impoverished. Not only was I worried about tuition fees every semester, but I also struggled to make ends meet on a daily basis. There was a time when I lived in other people's homes and gave private tutoring to earn tuition.

However, at that time, I and my peers clearly had the determination to live hard for a brighter future. In other words, with a 'hungry spirit,' we didn't give up on our hopes and dreams for the future, and even amidst the hardships, we managed to savor a bit of the romantic aspects of being a university student.

It has been 46 years since I entered university. In the meantime, we have gone through a tumultuous period of modernization, and Koreans have achieved what is known as the 'Miracle on the Han River,' significantly raising our standard of living.

We are now living in 2016, enjoying this affluence. It is unfortunate that, compared to the students of 46 years ago, we cannot find the same passion and romance in today's university students, who live in a time when our national average income and standard of living have improved so dramatically that it is difficult to even imagine what life was like back then.

Unlike the past when we ran with a 'hungry spirit,' believing that 'even if we're poor now, we can succeed if we work hard for tomorrow,' I feel sorry for the young people who are becoming frustrated amidst endless economic recession and worsening employment difficulties.

And when I hear news that prospective college students are already signing up for job preparation and certification courses as soon as they receive their acceptance letters, I feel more worried than sad. Aren't these young people the ones who will lead the future of our nation and the world?

In their 20s, especially as college students, it is a time when they should be designing their futures with big dreams. At a time when they should be developing their creative potential and challenging themselves with new endeavors to build their future, if our college students are solely focused on finding a stable job, then who will seek out and implement the development of our society?

Of course, finding a job and being economically active as a member of society is more important than anything else. However, if there is something even more important, it would be determining the direction of one's life. This is especially true considering how rapidly the world is changing.

Average life expectancy is increasing, but the term 'lifetime employment' has already disappeared. Even the average tenure at large companies is now only about 10 years. In this situation, the priority should be to consider what you want to do and how you want to live your life.

Rather than blindly seeking a stable job right in front of you, it is necessary to look at life from a broader perspective. Thinking about which certifications to obtain and which companies to apply to should be considered later.

Unlike our generation, who persevered with a mindset of having nothing left to lose, it might be difficult to expect courage and a bit of recklessness from today's young people who have grown up like greenhouse plants under their parents' care. However, once they realize that they are responsible for their own lives, I believe that today's young people, who have grown up in a global environment and are skilled in networking and communication, can definitely create change in ways that the older generation couldn't imagine.

It is very encouraging to hear that some young people with passion and vigor are not afraid of failure and are actively creating their own futures. Our society needs to support their endeavors.

Last year, a student from the university where I served as president sent me a message through Facebook. They shared their story about how they were trying to realize their dream of starting a business, but were hindered by the school's rules regarding the duration of leave of absence.

As soon as I heard this, I instructed the relevant department to review the matter and immediately establish a 'startup leave of absence system.' If I had been an old-fashioned person who only adhered to the rules, I might have been a major obstacle to that student's challenge.

However, if we can create small changes through smooth communication between the older and younger generations, won't there be more young people who are willing to break away from the status quo and explore new paths? Ultimately, this will be the driving force behind leading our society in a better direction.

Open minds are defined by its willingness to challenge

It's a tough world for people in their 20s. The employment barrier has become incredibly high, causing many young people to feel frustrated. However, we shouldn't forget that there are still students who are working hard to find new paths, even in difficult circumstances.

Nowadays, companies are said to require eight different specifications from job seekers: academic background, GPA, TOEIC score, certifications, language study experience, awards, internship experience, and volunteer activities. Even having one or two of these is challenging, so it's hard to imagine how difficult it is to find a job when all these conditions are required. This makes us realize just how severe the employment crisis is.

But no matter how difficult the situation, there's always a way to overcome it. If you think about what your unique strengths could be among countless competitors and work to develop them, you can definitely stand out. The most important virtue in this process is a challenging spirit. Anyone can come up with an idea, but not many people actually put it into action and challenge themselves.

Lee Won-bin, an economics student at Sogang University who swept various competitions with his own database, is one example of someone who has discovered unlimited possibilities. While juggling a busy academic schedule, Lee Won-bin's determination to delve into his areas of interest, develop ideas, and courageously take on challenges is truly commendable.

Contest: Soaring High

Interview with Lee Won—bin (Economics major, class of 10), a competition winner with a challenging spirit

Among the students who have been making remarkable achievements in various competitions, there is Lee Won-bin (Economics, Class of 10) who is still currently enrolled.

He won the grand prize at the "School Development Idea Award Ceremony" held on June 24, 2015, became one of the 20 winners out of 7,500 applicants for the "Wasakbasak (Crispy) Global Expedition Team (Wagledae) 1" trip to England, and received an honorable mention in the NH Nonghyup Life "Social Contribution Ideas College Student Contest."

Let's hear about the challenging spirit and unique competition know-how of this student who is now in his fourth year at the university.

Congratulations on winning first place in the recent SFC Idea Contest! Have you always been so passionate about improving our school?

Lee Won-bin: I'm actually a student designing my own major. I've noticed that many students are interested in creating their own majors, but they don't know it's an option and so they never pursue it. That's why I wanted to spread the word about student-designed majors.

When the school announced a contest, I saw it as a chance to expand on this idea with like-minded friends. My teammate was planning to design a major in applied statistics. It was great having so many friends around me who were also exploring their own unique academic paths, including real estate, anthropology, and applied statistics.

Congratulations on winning the Honorable Mention in the NH Nonghyup Life college competition! Can you tell me a bit about how you prepared your winning entry?

Lee Won-bin: This contest was right up my alley, as it aligned perfectly with my studies in actuarial science. The challenge was to propose a social contribution campaign based on one of two insurance design options provided by NH Nonghyup Life. I've always been interested in insurance products, so this was a great opportunity for me.

I teamed up with a friend who had interned at Allianz after winning a competition there, which definitely gave us an edge. Teamwork is crucial in any project, from brainstorming to the final presentation.

I've developed a habit of organizing my research and ideas into a personal database. When it comes to competitions like this, students need to convince companies that their ideas are worth investing in. But no matter how great your idea is, it's hard to persuade others without solid evidence.

I was able to leverage my experience from an Allianz project where I created a "Q-commerce curator." This tool allowed me to quickly gather and present the data I needed to support my proposal.

Congratulations on being chosen for the first SFC 'Wasakbasak Global Expedition'! You even got to go to England! What do you think made you stand out from all the other applicants?

Lee Won-bin: The "Wagledae" mission was a real time crunch. After making it to the top 100 out of 7,500 applicants, I had just two weeks to complete the final round, which involved creating a travel plan and proposing ideas for Hana Bank's growth.

The presentation for Hana Bank was particularly challenging, as I had to develop a comprehensive PowerPoint within a very short timeframe. I also struggled to come up with a unique theme for our 8-night, 9-day trip. Ultimately, I decided to repurpose some of my previous research on Allianz's character marketing.

While it took me almost a month to develop that initial plan, having the existing data made it much easier to create a strong argument and complete this new project in just two weeks. Although I wasn't entirely satisfied with the result, it was well-received and I won a spot on the trip to England!

Looking back, I think many teams had similar ideas, but my strong evidence set me apart. Having a well-organized database was a huge advantage in this situation.

I've noticed that you've done really well in various competitions and activities. What strategies do you use when writing your self-introductions or work plans?

Lee Won-bin: I believe in the power of a well-organized database. I have a system in place for storing self-introductions, PPT templates, and research materials. This makes it easy to repurpose content and jumpstart new projects. A robust database is also incredibly helpful for schoolwork. For example, when I took econometrics, I was able to leverage my existing templates, which my team found very useful.

When it comes to competitions, having a strong foundation of evidence is key. I can't stress enough the importance of building a database of resources.

Team composition is another critical factor. It's essential to have a team where members can complement each other's strengths. This prevents free-riding and fosters creativity.

As for self-introductions, I have a library of about 20 templates that I can customize for different applications. This allows me to continuously refine my self-presentation skills.[18]

---

18. Sogang University, SFC Newsletter, Vol. 296, July 9, 2013

Don't just look for a job, start your own business; aim higher.

Meanwhile, a growing number of students are pursuing entrepreneurship, fueled by their innovative ideas and skills. While student-led startups were once rare in Korea, the rise of smartphones and the Silicon Valley startup culture has inspired many young people to take the entrepreneurial leap. Although entrepreneurship is not yet considered a mainstream career path in our society, it's certainly admirable to see young people pursuing their passions with such vigor.

Sogang University's Startup Center has been at the forefront of fostering student entrepreneurship since 2014. Through initiatives like the annual Student Startup Competition, Startup Camps, mentoring programs, and the Sogang Start-Up Point System, the center provides students with the resources and support they need to turn their ideas into reality.

It is inevitable for students who have never experienced the real world outside of school to feel overwhelmed when trying to start a business, which involves finding ideas and recruiting team members. They constantly face questions that they cannot solve on their own, such as whether their ideas have market value or need further improvement.

To help students overcome these challenges and foster a more active startup ecosystem, Sogang University has been hosting a 'Student Startup Competition' since 2011. Through this competition, students can receive feedback on their ideas from a panel of professors and experts.

Winners not only receive prize money but also have the opportunity to receive mentoring on startup-related information and government startup support programs through the Sogang University Business Center. Additionally, they can receive ongoing support from on-campus organizations such as the industry-university cooperation foundation and technology holding company.

In January 2014, a new 'Startup-linked Major' was established to support aspiring student entrepreneurs. This unique Sogang University program allows students to combine two or more majors, fostering a multidisciplinary perspective.

Students who have a passion for entrepreneurship but lack the necessary technical or related knowledge can choose the 'Startup Major' as a second or third major. For example, an engineering student who takes business courses through the linked major can gain a comprehensive understanding of various aspects of starting a business, from product technology and manufacturing processes to marketing, sales, and management.

The startup major curriculum is structured to produce well-rounded entrepreneurs who possess both business acumen and technical skills, as well as strong communication and humanities skills. The curriculum is divided into three core areas: foundational knowledge, innovation and convergence, and entrepreneurship. To support student learning, the program offers mentorship from both faculty and industry experts, access to research facilities, and personalized mentorship.

Students no longer need to drop out of college to pursue their entrepreneurial dreams. Universities now provide structured support systems that can help students minimize risks and enhance their business skills.

While this is still a relatively new development, I believe that these initiatives will ultimately drive innovation and contribute to the growth of individuals, institutions, and society. The young people who are dedicating their time and energy to these endeavors are the ones who will shape the future.

Interview with the winner, Kim Tae-hoon

(Class of '04, Management), of the 3rd Sogang Startup Competition

1] What motivated you to choose entrepreneurship over employment?

I never really planned out my future into specific paths like employment, entrepreneurship, or civil service. I just followed my interests. For example, when I sold hotteok in front of the school, I did it because I enjoyed it, not because I had a goal of becoming a hotteok seller. The concept of "entrepreneurship" was foreign to me before I started my business.

As I explored my interests in school, I simply ended up doing what I loved. Even now, I feel like I'm continuing that same pattern, connecting my current passions with my past experiences. I guess you could say I'm a very curious person.

2] What was the toughest part about starting your own company?

The biggest challenge was learning to make decisions that affected others. Personally, I'm quite spontaneous, but as a leader, I had to consider the impact of my choices on my team. Every decision felt like a huge responsibility. It's taken about two years, but I'm finally starting to feel more confident in my decision-making process.

3] What was the inspiration behind your startup idea?

I was confused by the complexity of credit card options. The benefits were all about numbers and didn't seem to address my personal needs. I realized there was a gap in the market for a service that could help people find the right card based on their actual spending habits. That's why I started Banksalad

4] The impact Sogang University had on the decision to start a business

Sogang University has been the most influential place in my life, not just in my decision to start a business. It's like a second home to me. I believe that any success I have as an entrepreneur will be due to what I learned there. The university's emphasis on values and integrity has shaped my approach to business, from building a company to attracting talent. Instead of just giving you answers, Sogang teaches you how to think for yourself. This has allowed me to develop my own perspective and make sound decisions.

5] Advice for juniors considering starting a business

Ask questions, network, and take action. It's a shame how often we think about things but never do them. I believe that experience, not innate talent, is what sets people apart. Don't be afraid to ask for help—it won't cost you anything. And remember, acting impulsively doesn't always lead to negative consequences. In your 20s, it's better to learn from experience than to overthink things.

But make sure your actions align with your values, not just your desires[19].

19. Sogang University Official Blog, 1) 'I am a Sogang Person/Sogang Pride', 'Special Sogang, Special College Life 2): Embarking on Entrepreneurship: An Interview with Kim Tae-hoon (Business '04 Alumnus)', dated August 19, 2014.

In an era of studying failure!!
Let's break through closed systems
with challenges!

I recently heard from an acquaintance that they had participated in a 'Re-challenge Comeback Camp' hosted by the Ministry of Science and ICT and had gained a lot of courage. It was an event to support the re-challenge of venture company CEOs. However, I couldn't hide a slightly bitter feeling. I wondered why our society had been so harsh on people who had failed once that the government had to step in and hold a re-challenge camp.

Challenges are never easy. As the Chinese character for 'challenge' (挑戰) suggests, it means to face something head-on. If even one challenge is difficult, how much more so is it to challenge oneself again after failure? Those who re-challenge always have to fight against cold glances, poor environments, and financial difficulties.

However, we should never forget that our society grows by using failure as a foundation. Without failure, there is no success. It is meaningless to simply encourage people to 'try again.' The entire social system needs to change so that people can rise from failure. In Silicon Valley, the top investment priority for investors is companies that have failed twice. A country that has the power to challenge again is a country with a future.

Perhaps we could say that one's 20s are when people first experience 'failure.' After being protected within the confines of school during adolescence, they face college entrance exams and entering society, and for the first time, they taste the bitterness of life.

Most young people probably dream of a life without failure, where they achieve everything they desire and always succeed. And they work hard to make that happen. But does a life without failure actually exist?

In fact, it's much more common to achieve success based on the experience of failure. Rather than seeing failure as a setback, we should look for possibilities within it.

Recently, failure has become more than just a lesson; it has become a subject of research. 'Failure studies' have been applied in the field of management since the 1980s. 'Total Quality Management (TQM)' and 'Six Sigma,' which are still important in manufacturing today, are the results of efforts to reduce defects and make quality management easier. Global companies in the manufacturing industry always create failure analysis reports when developing products or improving quality. By analyzing the causes of failure and finding solutions, it ultimately becomes a driving force for innovation.

All the advanced technologies we enjoy today were born after countless failures. The reason why billions of won are invested in developing a new car is that it requires numerous trial and error to bring the safety of a vehicle with new features to a perfect level.

The pharmaceutical field is no different. It takes anywhere from 10 to 30 years to develop a new drug. Accumulated failures over those many years eventually lead to a single successful product.

Ultimately, we can say that a company's investment in research and development is an investment in failure.

The fact that major advanced countries have become space powers is also the result of continuously eliminating the causes of failure. In January 1986, the US space shuttle 'Challenger' exploded 73 seconds after launch, killing all seven crew members. It was confirmed that a single rubber gasket failed to function properly due to cold weather. The US used this experience to improve the perfection of its launch technology.

Not only in engineering, but also in the humanities and arts, there are countless examples of success after failure. Herman Melville, who wrote Moby-Dick, worked as a New York customs officer for 19 years while writing. However, he couldn't find a publisher to publish his books, so he had to self-publish and was always strapped for cash.

Walt Disney, the man who created the American Disney World myth, took the drawings he had created to a magazine company but was rejected. However, he didn't give up and continued to draw. One day, a mouse appeared in his studio, and Disney, thinking it was cute, gave it a piece of bread. He got inspiration from this.

Soon after, he produced his first animations, 'Lucky Rabbit' and 'Oswald.' While his first work was a commercial failure, Disney didn't give up and continued to draw the mouse he met in his studio. His persistence ultimately led to the creation of 'Mickey Mouse,' a beloved character among children, and today, it has created the global myth of Disneyland.

In the venture industry, which demands even more innovative

thinking, failure is utilized more actively. 'FailCon,' a 'failure conference' born in Silicon Valley, is a place where entrepreneurs discuss specific failure cases and get ideas from each other. It's essentially a gathering where venture entrepreneurs share their stories of failure and offer lessons like 'don't do this.'

This conference, centered around 'failure,' has been a huge success. First held in Silicon Valley in 2008, it has spread to Japan, Iran, and Spain. The conference's motto is 'Embrace failure and create success.'

CNN reported on the conference as a 'coming-out party for failures,' and the US public radio NPR introduced it as 'focused on the word "failure," which Silicon Valley loves.'

Chris DeWolfe, co-founder of MySpace, who attended the conference, confessed, 'Seeing those bizarre ads that encourage dieting made me realize I had lost control of my company.' Airbnb co-founder Joe Gebbia received cheers when he said, 'If people say, "Are you crazy?", it means you're doing it right.

Let's bring this back to our society. It's time for our society to change its perception of failure. Perhaps the reason why Korea's investment in R&D is lacking compared to other advanced countries is due to a social atmosphere that doesn't tolerate failure. However, we now live in an era of managing failure. If people in their 20s, who haven't even taken their first steps into society, become discouraged and give up after just a few failures, it's not only a personal misfortune but also a national waste. Creating a society that finds possibilities in failure and encourages those who have failed is the most urgent task for us right now.

Mistakes are unacceptable,
but failure is alright

Interview with Jung-hoon Yoo, CEO of Showbox Corp. Mediaplex and a driving force behind the Korean film industry (Business '83)

In 2012, our alum Dong-hoon Choi (Korean Lit '90) broke box office records with 'The Thieves,' raking in 12.98 million viewers. Behind this blockbuster is another Sogang alum, Showbox CEO Jung-hoon Yoo (Business '83). Yoo has been a driving force behind countless hits, including 'Nameless Gangster,' 'Detective K,' and 'The Man from Nowhere.' His company, Showbox, is a major player in the Korean film industry, distributing over ten films a year.

I asked him about the most successful and unsuccessful cases among the countless films that Showbox has invested in and distributed. However, before using the terms 'success' and 'failure,' CEO Jung-hoon Yoo wanted to clarify what those terms meant to him. He said, 'If we simply define success and failure based on box office performance, then the top 1, 2, and 3 box office hits would be the most successful cases, and the bottom 1, 2, and 3 would be the most unsuccessful. However, I don't want to define success and failure in that way. Every time I invest in a film, I set my own criteria and goals, and based on that, I determine whether it was a 'success' or whether I have 'regrets'.

For CEO Jung-hoon Yoo, the most successful film was 'The Thieves.' It wasn't just because of its box office success, but also because it achieved all the goals he had set out to accomplish. He had long wanted to work with director Dong-hoon Choi and break Korea's box office records together. They collaborated on ideas, cast actors, and developed a new marketing strategy. The result was a huge success. Despite the numerous Hollywood blockbusters released that year, 'The Thieves' emerged as the biggest sensation. Yoo also revealed that he is preparing for an even bigger project this year, building on the success of 'The Thieves.'

On the other hand, he cited 'Barefooted Dream' as the film he regretted the most. 'Barefooted Dream,' a human drama about a former soccer player who forms a soccer team with children in war-torn East Timor, was released in 2010 and attracted about 400,000 viewers. Although it was a small-scale film, the project started to deviate from its initial goals, and eventually, marketing and distribution also failed to meet their objectives. Although the film received positive reviews from those who watched it, he has many regrets about the overall outcome.

"However, I believe that while mistakes should be avoided, failure is okay. When I say that mistakes should be avoided, it means that I haven't been thorough enough. On the other hand, failure means that I haven't achieved my goal despite my intentions. Failure at least leaves us with lessons, and it leads to future successes. Although I was disappointed with the outcome of 'Barefooted Dream,' it's a film that I'm grateful for because it taught me how to avoid making the same mistakes in the future"[20].

20. Sogang University's SFC Newsletter, Vol. 288, May 14, 2013

Dreaming of the birth
of a Korean Steve Jobs...

As mentioned earlier, South Korea's education system, which separates students into humanities and science tracks from high school and continues this division through university, is no longer sustainable. In an era where products born from the fusion of engineering and humanities are gaining attention, this system is clearly outdated.

In fact, interdisciplinary studies are being widely utilized not only in academia but also in the business world. To keep up with these global trends, education must change. Engineers who don't understand business and business majors who don't know philosophy can no longer stay ahead.

Sogang University's Interdisciplinary Studies Department, with its 'Art & Technology' major, was established to address this changing landscape. 1 First admitting students in March 2012, the department aims to cultivate individuals capable of interdisciplinary studies. It is modeled after Carnegie Mellon University's Entertainment Technology Center.

To facilitate interdisciplinary studies, the Art & Technology major has established a new educational system that creatively integrates humanistic imagination, cultural and artistic sensibility, and advanced engineering. With the slogan 'Creation, Beyond

Imagination,' the core of the Art & Technology curriculum lies in conducting fusion projects based on understanding creative ideas, methods of expression, and implementation technologies through intuition and insight.

Through this educational system, students can undertake projects closely linked to industrial sites. Additionally, a motivating mentoring system is in place, allowing students to receive practical insights and field experience from experts, enhancing their understanding of industrial settings.

It is often said that two personalities coexist within our minds. The left and right hemispheres of the human brain, while overlapping in many functions, also perform distinctly different specialized roles. The left brain is responsible for logic, rationality, and language functions, while the right brain is responsible for emotion, creativity, visual functions, and social skills.

Individuals who can effectively utilize both the left and right brains are those with the integrated capabilities sought after by the Art & Technology major. This major was created with the dream of fostering Korea's own Steve Jobs. Unlike traditional majors, it is a new educational system that transcends disciplinary boundaries, creatively integrating humanistic imagination, cultural and artistic sensibility, and advanced engineering.

We are now in an era of large-scale research and converging technologies. This convergence is not only occurring between various scientific and technological fields but also between science and technology, arts, humanities, and social sciences.

From a sociocultural perspective, as the value of life shifts from material to human values, interest in emotional well-being, culture, entertainment, and interpersonal and social relationships has increased. Meanwhile, from a national economic standpoint, transitioning to an economic system based on the cultural industry, creative research, and innovative products and new industries has emerged as a national policy goal.

These changes mean that there is a growing demand for research on science and technology that enhances human capabilities and the value of life, rather than focusing on groundbreaking inventions or machines. Moreover, in this era of converging technology industries where value is generated and competitiveness is formed from culture, arts, and content, the understanding that technology should not exist solely as technology but should be user-friendly and enjoyable is spreading through the humanities.

As interdisciplinary knowledge and studies become more prevalent, the imagination cultivated by the humanities and the sensitivity generated through art are recognized as essential abilities for 21st-century individuals. Future talent cultivated through the Art & Technology major will contribute to enhancing the nation's capabilities through technological and cultural innovation and the industrialization of the humanities, while also enriching the future of humanity.

Your 20s are a time of open opportunities. Discover what truly drives you

As former U.S. President Obama once praised, South Korea's educational fervor is world-class. In an increasingly competitive society where families are having fewer children, the educational zeal has extended to even infants. Following expensive English kindergartens, play schools before kindergarten are now considered essential for child education. This is a stark contrast to our childhood when playing joyfully with neighborhood friends on the dirt was enough to be happy.

The problem lies in the fact that most of these educational methods are driven by parents and teachers, gradually eroding children's autonomy. As a result, many students who have simply followed instructions throughout high school experience a significant shock when they enter university. They become frustrated when they can't rely on academies or textbooks for help when they don't understand a professor's lecture during class, and they wander aimlessly before graduation, not knowing what or how to prepare. Eventually, they end up following the crowd and focusing on 'building up their specs,' once again turning to academies for help.

To set a direction in life and courageously pursue it, adequate preparation is necessary. Blindly challenging something without any preparation can only be seen as recklessness, not courage. So, what and how should we prepare?

First, it is necessary to understand oneself. Bernard Werber, a famous French novelist known for his works such as Ants and The Brain, states that a failed life is one where a person lives to satisfy others rather than living according to their own will.

No matter how socially recognized, if one is not satisfied and happy, life can be miserable. Finding out what you want and what you want to do is the first thing you should do.

Once you've found out what you want to do, you need to develop your own strengths. What's needed here is an objective view of oneself. You need to carefully consider what you're good at, what you lack, and what you need more of and can develop. Observing others and listening to what they say can help you understand yourself better. Instead of comparing yourself to others and becoming arrogant or self-deprecating, you need a perspective that allows you to objectify yourself and see yourself as you are. That is the open-minded spirit that 20-year-olds should have.

Once you've figured out what you want to do and what skills you need to develop, the next step is to fill in the gaps. While everyone's needs will vary, there's one thing that's universally beneficial: reading. The importance of reading cannot be overstated. Nothing stimulates the brain like reading. Input is necessary for output. Without any input, fresh ideas cannot be generated.

To read effectively, I recommend creating your own summary files. Rather than summarizing the entire book, extract the most impactful parts, the ones you want to remember, and write them down separately. It's virtually impossible to remember everything you read. By creating your own database through reading, you'll have a valuable source of ideas for a long time.

I also want to emphasize the importance of foreign languages. With the development of the internet connecting the world, access to information is limitless. However, without proficiency in English, the global lingua franca, your access will be significantly limited. You should learn a foreign language not for exams, but for real-life use and necessity.

Language learning requires consistent effort, as it cannot be achieved through cramming. Giving up because you lack confidence will mean missing out on future opportunities. Learning languages like Chinese or German, in addition to English, can also broaden your perspective by introducing you to new cultures and customs.

Interview with Lawyer Kim Chang-hoon (Philosophy '01), who turned his passion into reality

From music to law, Kim Chang-hoon (Philosophy '01) has had quite a journey. After pursuing his passion for music, including performing with indie bands, he unexpectedly passed the bar exam while still in university. Let's hear his inspiring story.

Could you please introduce yourself first?

Yes, my name is Kim Chang-hoon, and I graduated from the

Philosophy department in 2001. I'm currently a lawyer at Jeongsang Law Firm

I heard you were a vocalist for Kinziex. Have you always been interested in music?

While I've always been interested in band activities, I had to focus on my college entrance exams during high school. So, I made it my goal to join a band club as soon as I got to university. With the dream of becoming a vocalist, I practiced singing very hard throughout my senior year of high school and even during my gap year. At the time, I thought the vocalist was the centerpiece of a band. (laughs) I was so happy when I finally joined Kinziex, my dream band, after entering Sogang University!

Then, what is the most memorable thing that happened while you were active in Kinziex?

The most memorable experience was during my time in the 27th generation, when we struggled to recruit members all year. Even though we had many performances, I felt a bit regretful that we couldn't complete the full band lineup.

I was also excited and nervous when we performed in front of a large audience at freshman orientation. Since we worked so hard, I wanted to promote Sogang University by participating in the college music festival. We prepared and participated, but unfortunately, we were eliminated in the second round.

Later, the 30th generation advanced to the finals and even

appeared on the terrestrial TV show "Show! Music Core".

I heard you were also active as an indie band at the underground entertainment places near Hongik University. I'm curious about how that happened.

Anyone can join an indie band in the underground music scene near Hongik University. After serving in the military, I really wanted to be in a band and I wanted to be good at it. So, I decided to give it a shot because I knew I would regret it if I didn't. Since it was something I truly wanted to do, I searched online for people around my age who shared similar musical tastes and auditioned for various bands. The band I joined, Makchangdan, was relatively new and was missing a vocalist. I was in the band for about a year.

Although I wasn't particularly skilled at composing or writing lyrics, I tried my best and ended up writing and composing many songs based on melodies I would hum while playing the guitar. I participated in many competitions and won quite a few awards. When money was tight, I would participate in indie band competitions to earn prize money to support myself.

During my time with Kinziex, we needed to hold regular performances, which required a few million won. Since we had no budget, I would create original songs and enter competitions to earn money. It was satisfying to win awards for my own songs.

However, as I participated in more competitions with larger audiences, I realized that there were so many talented people in the world. The music industry was incredibly competitive. There were people who were so passionate about music. Being surrounded by such talented individuals, I felt a bit intimidated. I thought to myself, "Now, that's a real musician."

So, did you change your career path to become a judicial examination candidate?

After the indie band I was in disbanded, I experienced a period of significant personal growth. Needing to find a new path, I observed what others were doing. Many were preparing for the CPA exam, but I lacked confidence in that route.

I yearned to do something meaningful, but my limited English proficiency made me hesitant about job hunting, and my only notable experience was being in a band. However, I had a romantic notion of passing the judicial examination. I thought that even though I was starting late, I should at least give it a shot while I was young.

I also had a desire to stand up for the underprivileged. Just as music should be accessible to everyone, I believed the law should be applied equally to all. With the hope of making a small contribution to that goal, I decided to take on the challenge of the judicial examination.

Can you recall any favorite classes or professors from your days at Sogang?

I remember Professor Choi Jin-seok from my philosophy class. It was an Eastern philosophy course. He probably doesn't remember me (laughs), but he once said in class, 'People who study philosophy can do anything.' That statement really stuck with me. I think it's why I was able to both be in a band and study for the judicial examination.

You must have worked incredibly hard. Can you tell me exactly when you started preparing for the judicial examination and when you finally passed?

I started preparing for the judicial examination in November 2006, packing my bags and moving into a small apartment near the school. I hardly saw any friends and immersed myself completely in my studies, living the life of a law school examinee. Although I occasionally went out for drinks, I spent most of my time studying.

In June 2007, with the mindset of "If you want to catch a tiger, you have to go into the tiger's den," I took a leave of absence and moved to Sinlim-dong, a neighborhood known for its law school exam cram schools. I stayed in Sinlim-dong until June 2009, after taking the second exam. When I left, I packed everything up with the determination to never do it again.

I passed the first exam in February 2008 but struggled with the second exam subjects, which were completely new to me. I attended a cram school for only three months and took the second exam in June of the same year, but unfortunately, I failed.

Since I was allowed to take the second exam the following year after passing the first, I took it again in 2009 and passed. I received the final passing notice during my last semester of university. Ironically, I got a C in Criminal Law III that semester, even though it was a law course I took after passing the exam.

What strategies did you use to pass the bar exam in such a short time, considering you didn't have a law background?

There's a common belief that anyone can pass the bar exam by attending a cram school and consistently reviewing the material. However, I wanted to pass as quickly as possible, and given my age, I needed to save time. I also thought that I couldn't succeed if I did the same thing as everyone else.

If I had attended a cram school, I felt like I would just be following the curriculum without really understanding the material. So, I decided to study independently by gathering materials from various cram schools.

Except for the three months I spent at a cram school for the second exam subjects, which were completely unfamiliar to me, I studied entirely on my own. I studied alone for 15 hours a day without a single break. Although it was challenging and exhausting, I found that self-study was a more effective way for me to learn.

For our younger students who may be feeling lost about their future, what advice would you give them?

I'm feeling lost myself, to be honest. (laughs) Life isn't as simple as just getting a job and everything falling into place.

However, as long as you're young and passionate, I believe you can take on any challenge. If you approach it with sincerity, believe in yourself, and give it your all, I'm confident you'll achieve great results[21].

---

21. Sogang University, SFC Newsletter, Volume 302, dated August 20, 2013

Chapter 5

Leaders of an Open System

When I asked students about their dreams
during their entrance interviews,
I was surprised to find that only about 20%
could clearly articulate their goals. 20-30% didn't have any dreams at all,

and the rest were uncertain.
Isn't it true that something you can passionately
pursue even late into the night is a dream?
How can we expect to cultivate 'creative' individuals
when they are so unsure about their future?

*- Lee Jin-soo, Director of the Future IT Convergence Research Institute at
 POSTECH*

Beyond boundaries: Innovation through Openness

Pioneers who have practiced open systems

Park Ji-sung, a pride of Korean soccer, represents
the open system of the sports world as a versatile player.
SoftBank Chairman Masayoshi Son is an open system leader
in the business world,
looking 300 years into the future rather than just 30.
I hope that through the open leaders around us,
more leaders will emerge who can break through
common sense and limitations to create new innovations.

An Open System in the World of Soccer:
The Versatile Park Ji-sung

Never backing down in the face of adversity, Son Masayoshi is a leader of an open system who overturns common sense and turns the tide. In 2001, when he challenged NTT Docomo, Japan's leading telecommunications company, in the ADSL business and faced the seemingly insurmountable obstacle of being unable to lease optical cables, he resorted to dramatic tactics to draw attention to the issue and force a resolution. Also, when the IT bubble burst the previous year and his company's market capitalization plummeted, he personally conducted a marathon six-hour explanation session at the annual shareholders' meeting, patiently addressing their concerns.

Instead of just looking up to Steve Jobs, let's cultivate our own 'Son Masayoshi'—a world-class leader who defies conventions and drives innovation. To do that, we need to go beyond common sense and nurture a spirit of bold, unconventional thinking.

The concept of a multi-player, someone who can naturally adapt to any role, reminds me of an open system that breaks down boundaries and creates new value. While specialized skills are valuable, a friend who excels in science but also has interests and talents in humanities, philosophy, music, and art has endless possibilities and is an absolutely necessary talent in society.

If Park Ji-sung was only good at attacking, he wouldn't have thrived

as a national team player. Park Ji-sung's versatility was exceptional; few players, even under the famously flexible Sir Alex Ferguson, were utilized in so many different positions. He played as a left-wing midfielder, a right-wing midfielder, a winger, an attacking midfielder, a central midfielder, and even a defensive midfielder at Manchester United.

Shouldn't our young people also strive to become multi-players who can transcend various fields?

We shouldn't shy away from a sales role just because we dislike meeting people. The task given to us is an opportunity. We should confront it and find our own path. If we give up from the beginning, society will never look for that young person again.

If a company needs someone to handle various management tasks, such as sales, production, and distribution, a multi-player who can fill that gap without requiring additional hires would be invaluable.

When a multi-player in football takes on a new position, we see that they are not simply extending their play; a winger and a central midfielder, for example, have different roles and require different approaches. Even experienced wingers, when moved to central midfield, must adapt and adopt a new approach.

Similarly, in the real world, it would be the smoothest path to stick to one's major and reach the top in that field. However, the world doesn't always work according to calculations.

Therefore, we must be prepared so that our dreams are not shattered by any unexpected variables. We must be willing to boldly abandon our habits and patterns. Only then can we easily accept and adapt to different positions. Abandoning habits is the first step to an open system. By discarding past habits, we can receive new value.

An Open System in Business:
SoftBank's Masayoshi Son

Looking 300 years into the future, Son Masayoshi, a Korean-Japanese entrepreneur who rivals Bill Gates and Steve Jobs in the cutting-edge IT industry, is an inspiration to young entrepreneurs with his groundbreaking, open-minded spirit. Unlike others who might plan 30 years ahead, he envisions how much revenue his company will generate and in what business it will be 300 years from now.

He doesn't just anticipate future trends; he actively shapes them through bold investments and strategic initiatives. Few global business leaders strategize over even 4 or 5 generations, let alone 300 years.

Standing on a citrus box in a meager office with an old fan, Son Masayoshi proclaimed that in 30 years, his company, SoftBank, would achieve trillions of yen in sales. This was September 1981, and SoftBank had just opened its doors in a shabby two-story building in Oodori, Fukuoka, with only two employees. His passionate, almost dream-like speech, however, led his two employees to quit within two months. Everyone looked at Son and SoftBank with skepticism.

Despite the initial skepticism, some people recognized his passion and genius, including Sasaki, an executive at Sharp, one of Japan's leading electronics companies. He mortgaged his own house to lend money to Son, who then managed to secure an exclusive contract with Hudson, Japan's largest software company. Through this, SoftBank instantly jumped to become a mid-sized company with 3.5 billion yen in sales. In 1983, Weekly Asahi introduced him as a 'monster businessman'.

Revealed in August 2010, Son Masayoshi's remarkable 50-year life plan provides further insight into his strategic mindset. "In my 20s, I went to the battlefield to make a name for myself. In my 30s, I raised funds. In my 40s, I made the biggest gamble of my life. In my 50s, I completed my business. So, in my 60s, I will hand over the business to the next generation." Having meticulously followed this plan without a single misstep so far, it is expected that he will continue to do so in the future.

Never backing down in the face of adversity, Son Masayoshi is a leader of an open system who overturns common sense and turns the tide. In 2001, when he challenged NTT Docomo, Japan's leading telecommunications company, in the ADSL business and faced the seemingly insurmountable obstacle of being unable to lease optical cables, he resorted to dramatic tactics to draw attention to the issue and force a resolution. Also, when the IT bubble burst the previous year and his company's market capitalization plummeted, he personally conducted a marathon six-hour explanation session at the annual shareholders' meeting, patiently addressing their concerns.

Instead of just looking up to Steve Jobs, let's cultivate our own 'Son Masayoshi'—a world-class leader who defies conventions and drives innovation. To do that, we need to go beyond common sense and nurture a spirit of bold, unconventional thinking.

Determined to study in the United States, 17-year-old Son Masayoshi set his sights on learning about advanced civilizations. However, his family's financial situation was precarious due to his father's worsening illness. Despite this, Son insisted on pursuing his goal. He withdrew from school and tirelessly persuaded his family and relatives until he secured the necessary funds.

His unwavering determination in the face of immediate difficulties and his passionate drive to pursue his dreams and open up the future exemplify the entrepreneurial spirit that defines the 21st century. Or perhaps, it's not necessary to limit it to the 21st century. Perhaps this forward-thinking attitude is the 'old future' of humanity.

An Open System in Employment:
Jobs that Challenge Conventional Wisdom

If you do the same as everyone else, you can't get ahead; everyone complains about how hard it is to find a job, but it's difficult precisely because everyone prepares the same way. An open system starts with rejecting norms and patterns. Sending a resume to the company you want to work for via email is a conventional approach.

Will that ordinary method open the door to that company? The method must be different, and your mindset must be different too. To stand out, you need to break the mold. I remember an advertisement where a person climbed down a rope from the roof of a building to submit a resume.

While that might be a bit exaggerated, you need that level of passion to get a job, don't you? While specs and grades are important, I'm particularly drawn to candidates with exceptional passion and drive. If you have that, I want to interview you first."

Kim Hee-jung lacked any 'official certifications' or 'completion certificates for professional courses,' but she desperately wanted to work for the PR team of a cosmetics company. She sent nearly 100 emails to the PR team, and one day, she received a call for an interview. She later learned that the PR team leader had printed out all her emails and 'was waiting for me.'

In a human society, we need to open closed doors with humanity.

Simply using gimmicks won't attract attention. Companies want sincere and passionate people. You shouldn't simply send a resume via email. You should write a handwritten letter or think of another unique way to convey your sincere desire to work for that company.

Job doors cannot be opened with just specifications; nowadays, it's better to utilize job performance evaluations. Job performance evaluations based on NCS (National Competency Standards) are a positive system that shifts from specification-based hiring to ability-based hiring. There's a saying that college students spend 40 million won building their specifications. That's a significant investment, especially considering that companies reportedly spend nearly 60 million won to cultivate the talents they recruit into employees with job performance capabilities.

While students invest heavily in building their specifications, companies also face significant costs in training new hires. Wouldn't a more efficient and equitable employment system be created if we could reduce the gap between these two?

Job performance evaluation is a fundamental element of an open employment system that opens up the current closed job market.

Companies are changing, with SK Group taking a significant step towards eliminating the reliance on specifications in their hiring process starting this fall. They've completely removed specification-related items from their job application forms. Applicants are also no longer allowed to attach their photos. By only requiring basic information like education, major, and GPA, they emphasize self-introductions and interviews.

Similarly, Hyosung Group verifies the compatibility between applicants and the company, as well as their numerical, verbal, and logical reasoning abilities, through aptitude tests. Interviews are conducted in a deep evaluation format consisting of job presentations, core value competency interviews, and group discussions.

In contrast, CJ Group's Comprehensive Ability Test (CAT) is unique in that there are no separate sections. Questions are presented all at once, covering areas such as applicants' humanities knowledge, verbal reasoning, numerical reasoning, and spatial perception. Applicants have to answer 95 questions in 60 minutes. For the personality test, they need to answer 250 questions in 40 minutes.

I believe it's more important to figure out what you like doing and what skills you have, rather than focusing on increasing your TOEIC score by 100 points—that's the foundation of an open employment system. Gain experience, explore the world, and create your own story instead of blindly accumulating specifications. Companies hire people who can do the job well, not people who are just good at presenting a polished facade.

I was deeply impressed by what a certain talented person said about breaking the norms of employment. They said, 'A football team has 11 players, and each has their own position. No matter how many great goalkeepers there are, the coach won't put three goalkeepers on the field at once.

Instead of following others and focusing solely on specifications like TOEIC scores, if you find your own competitive edge and do your best, you can be placed in a good position.'

An Open System in STEM Fields:
Attracting Genius STEM Talent

Many have wondered why Koreans have yet to win a Nobel Prize. Especially in the field of science, when will we see a Nobel laureate? Of course, whether or not we win an award isn't the most important thing, but it's worth looking into the issues facing Korean science. It seems like our scientific community faces challenges with collaboration, interdisciplinary research, and embracing new ideas. This perceived closed-off nature may be hindering our ability to advance and make groundbreaking discoveries.

In 2008, I was envious of Japanese science, especially when their physicists won the Nobel Prize in Physics. Why couldn't Korea do the same? Beyond envy, I felt a deep sense of regret. What was the difference between Korea and Japan?

The most fundamental difference was our attitude towards accepting new knowledge. Through the Meiji Restoration, Japan opened up the entire nation to the world. To put it simply, the Meiji Restoration was about the attitude of accepting and absorbing anything good to upgrade the nation qualitatively. Isn't it from that point that the gap between Korea and Japan widened? I think the qualitative difference in science also began at that point.

Japanese science embraced not just the finished product of Western knowledge, but also the methods for creating that knowledge. They were not content with simply studying advanced science; they actively engaged in research to contribute to its advancement.

While I acknowledge that we started later than Japan, I refuse to accept that we can never catch up—that's not the spirit of Sogang. That's why I've been thinking about attracting talent. Just as a star player can transform a team, I believe our scientific community needs individuals who can inspire and drive innovation. Are there such talents within South Korea? I think we need to look beyond our borders and seek out Korean scientific talent working in leading research institutions around the world. We should actively recruit these talents and quickly apply their advanced scientific know-how to our scientific community.

There are many Indian, Chinese, and Japanese scientists in the

United States, but few Koreans. This is likely because the roots of domestic science are weak, preventing us from expanding globally. The treatment of science and engineering fields in countries like the US and Germany is vastly different.

Reversing this situation in a short period is impossible. It would require significantly reforming our current education system, which is a daunting task.

However, the United States offers a potential model: it's a country where scientific talents of all races gather. Why can't Korea foster a similarly welcoming and inclusive environment?

Korea has historically relied on imports when lacking resources, even exporting people to build our nation's wealth. We built our nation's wealth on labor rather than intellect. Diligence was our weapon. However, those days are over. Now is the era of brains, not brawn. If we need something, we can import it. It's like recruiting star players in professional sports. When a star player joins a team, the domestic players upgrade their skills by observing their techniques. Similarly, by attracting top scientific talent, we can elevate our entire research community

Instead of recognizing the immense scientific potential of China and India, why don't we invite their scientific talents? Furthermore, why don't we create an environment where European or American talents can play a role in Asia?

If Korea failed to open up 100 years ago and fell behind Japan, then we should open our doors now and let high-level talents inject new ideas and perspectives into our scientific community. I believe that would be the beginning of an open system in science and engineering.

The Korean scientific community needs rapid growth, just as the Korean economy experienced rapid, compressed growth. To achieve this, I believe we should recruit high-level talents and use them as a catalyst for innovation and growth.

The Open System of the Internet:
The Internet of Things

It seems like South Korea is a step ahead of the rest of the world when it comes to the internet. From semiconductors to optical networks, our infrastructure is more than sufficient. However, to truly harness the power of this infrastructure, software development is crucial. For our internet to develop further, we need to create innovative software and applications.

Modern apartments in Korea offer a glimpse into the future of connected living. High-speed telecommunications and home networks have reached a point where you can control everything—lighting, temperature, appliances—with a single button. This seamless integration of technology into everyday life is a significant advantage that Korea is well-positioned to capitalize on.

The term most frequently mentioned in relation to the combination of apartments and the internet is the "Internet of Things."

The Internet of Things (IoT) refers to a network of physical devices, vehicles, home appliances, and other items embedded with electronics, software, sensors, actuators, and network connectivity. This enables these objects to connect and exchange data.

The term was first used in 1999 by Kevin Ashton, director of the Auto-ID Center at the Massachusetts Institute of Technology. He

predicted that the Internet of Things would be built by embedding RFID tags and other sensors in everyday objects. Since then, the term has become widely used in market analysis materials[22].

Having passed through the Industrial Revolution and the Information Revolution, our society is now entering the era of the hyperconnected revolution, where all things are interconnected.

People, objects, spaces, and data are connected through the internet, becoming the foundation of our lives. From Busan, you can control the gas in your home in Seoul, and the refrigerator's software can tell you vocally about the level of food spoilage inside. Simply looking in the mirror, it might advise you on what to wear based on today's weather.

---

22. Naver Knowledge Encyclopedia, Korea: Internet of Things [Internet of Things (IoT), things-], Refer to (Doosan Encyclopedia, Korea)

While this may sound like something out of a movie, it's already becoming a reality around us. This is the open-system revolution, the Internet of Things, that the internet is bringing about.

How did we meet computers? Early computers were far from instant; we relied on floppy disks and CDs, and boot times were long. Even with the advent of USBs and iPads, we've only recently begun to fully embrace the digital age. However, compared to other countries, our information revolution was incredibly fast. But future progress hinges on our ability to harness the potential of the Internet of Things.

Even my car now has Bluetooth service. I can make calls without picking up my phone and listen to music from my phone. Although I'm a bit old-fashioned, I'm gradually getting used to these IoT services. I might even start using a smartwatch or a home assistant soon.

Until now, for devices connected to the internet to exchange information, human 'operation' was required. In the era of the Internet of Things, devices can exchange information and communicate without human intervention, using technologies like Bluetooth, Near Field Communication (NFC), sensor data, and networks.

As mentioned earlier, Korea has a unique environment of internet and apartments, and I am convinced that applying the Internet of Things to apartments will spark an amazing lifestyle revolution. Perhaps some construction companies are already experimenting and researching this. Apartments are the most popular housing culture in Korea. Few countries have embraced the internet as rapidly and thoroughly as Korea. By maximizing this unique advantage with the Internet of Things, we could see a global shift in how we design and interact with our living spaces.

Open Systems in Everyday Life:
30 Tips for an Open System

1. An open family system
Frequently switch the roles of husband and wife. Nowadays, husbands who cook are cooler.

2. An open system of youth
Create your own boundaries in your own way. Be an Only One, not one of them.

3. An open university system
Don't just stay within the universities of South Korea. The classroom is already open to the outside world.

4. An open employment system
Don't look for a job the same way you did 10 years ago. Approach interviews with a desire to show something new.

5. An open administrative system
Go beyond the public and private sectors. We need flying ideas, not just stagnant bureaucracy.

6. An open national system
Abandon the idea that your nation is the best. The whole world is already one nation.

7. An open trend system
9 out of 10 people open a chicken restaurant. Why not become a chicken restaurant consultant instead?

8. An Open System in Food

Korea is the only country in the world that has the ingenious dish called Bibimbap. It's a bowl of rice mixed with all sorts of vegetables, a spoonful of gochujang (Korean chili paste), sesame oil, and a fried egg. Bibimbap is an open system, an integration, and a fusion. By mixing all these ingredients, we get a completely different taste and nutrition. That's the open system of food.

9. Oda Nobunaga's Open System

Oda Nobunaga, encountering a Portuguese shipwrecked by a storm, introduced matchlocks and learned from them, laying the foundation for Japan to become a powerful nation.

10. Copernicus' Open System

A resistance to the absolute. The Earth had to give up its immense privilege of being the center of the universe. Humanity faced a tremendous crisis. Beliefs in religion, holiness, and a sinless world were on the verge of becoming mere dreams due to Copernicus.

11. An Open System of Humor

Humor is a device that opens closed systems. The world opens up when we laugh.

12. An Open System of Language

 English is not everything. Open up to other worlds through languages other than English. Acquiring a unique language and becoming a unique presence in that world is also a way.

13. An Open System of Gender

Men should challenge women's domains, and women should challenge men's domains.

14. An Open System of Mathematics

Don't confine mathematics to the classroom. Find mathematics in everyday life. You can find connections between mathematics and movies, literature, and even dieting.

15. An Open System of History
Question history. Seek out the history that has been hidden or distorted by those in power.

16. An Open System of Entrepreneurship
Start a business alone instead of with a partner. Start a business alone and then partner with others.

17. An Open System of Campus Life
Don't think that studying is only done on campus. Don't just passively receive information, actively seek out knowledge. Go out and learn.

18. An Open System of Travel
Don't always travel to the same places. Instead of following the crowd, embark on a journey with your own unique concept.

19. An Open System of Reading
Change your reading patterns. If you're in the humanities, try reading science books. Conversely, if you're in STEM, delve into literature and writing.

20. An Open System of Talent
Instead of hiring people who excel in one area, seek out creative, fusion-type multi-talented individuals.

21.An Open System of Residence
Don't be fixated on Seoul. Don't be limited to your own country. Shift the focus of your life to the provinces and the world.

22. An Open System of Education
Break away from the conventional wisdom about education. Develop your abilities, not just your academic credentials.

23. An Open System of Ideology

Embrace and listen to ideas that are different from your own. Abandon the belief that your ideology is superior.

24. An Open System of Markets

Disrupt the conventional wisdom of the market. Pioneer a blue ocean of marketing that others haven't explored.

25.An Open System in Marriage

There should be no secrets between a husband and wife. Let's live honestly with each other. That's how relationships last.

26. An Open System of Nations

Let's not just stay in one country. Let's try living in other countries. Different circumstances open up your mind.

27.An Open System of Art

Combine science and art. Combine architecture and music.

28. An Open System of Friendship

Make friends with foreigners. Make friends from different countries.

29. An Open System of Society

Look at the suffering of those below you more than those above you, and lend a helping hand. Harmony in living well together is an open revolution towards a better society than the competition of living well alone.

30. An Open System of Age

Throw away your preconceived notions about age and numbers. Learn from children, and be confident in front of adults. The elderly are a history of wisdom, and children are seeds of new beginnings.

Epilogue

Once upon a time, a grandfather and his grandson were planting beans in a field. The young grandson treated each seed with great care, planting one seed at a time. However, the grandfather was planting three seeds in each hole. Curious, the grandson asked, "Grandpa, why are you wasting seeds by planting three at a time?" The grandfather's reply was a masterpiece. "One seed will be eaten by a bird flying in the sky, one by a bug crawling on the ground, and the remaining one will be eaten by a person," he said. It was a story he had heard from his grandmother a long time ago.

This simple tale offers a glimpse into the fundamental mindset of farmers. I was reminded of this story recently when I read a piece by the late literary critic, Lee O-young. He interpreted this story in relation to the philosophy of Heaven, Earth, and Man, where there was a natural and cyclical communication between them. He discussed the wisdom of the ancients. How did the ancients come to understand the universal order contained in a tiny bean? Thinking about how they planted beans with open hearts towards heaven, earth, and humanity, I am deeply moved. Perhaps the old ethics of sharing and giving were also related to this open wisdom.

However, it is also true that such open-heartedness has not always prevailed throughout history. Instead of communicating openly and joining forces, people often formed factions and engaged in conflicts. Closed-minded partisan struggles frequently endangered the fate of the nation. The isolationist policy of the late Joseon Dynasty is a prime example. If a more progressive and open attitude had been maintained then, our modern history might have unfolded differently.

Despite experiencing various periods of openness and closure throughout our 5,000-year history, we are still not free from the confines of blood ties, regionalism, and school ties. We have often suffered unnecessarily because we were excessively lenient towards selfish connections and overly strict with altruistic communication. While the closed mindset of settled communities can bring stability and peace on the one hand, it can also lead to stagnation and decline. As the saying goes, stagnant water is prone to rot.

I have spent my entire life as an engineer. To enrich and advance human civilization and life through advancements in science and technology, engineers cannot afford to stagnate. They must constantly strive for new developments and inventions, rather than resting on their laurels. Therefore, it is imperative for engineers to maintain an open, rather than a closed, mindset. They must become digital nomads equipped with an open nomadic spirit. If someone were to say, "I have already developed this technology," and emphasize a closed-minded sense of pride, they would have strayed far from the path of a true engineer.

However, after over 30 years of teaching engineering, I have realized that the walls of reality are very thick. I have often witnessed people living in closed societies, trapped within their own personal walls. During my time as a university president, I had many opportunities to reflect on the university and society as a whole. Without a doubt, I observed alarming signs of closure in both our university and society at large. It was truly unfortunate and regrettable.

As an engineering professor and a university president, I have always aspired to cultivate open-minded young people through open education, so that they can contribute to our nation and the world. However, the walls of reality seemed stubbornly persistent.

That's why I wanted to propose the 'Open System' project, drawing on the wisdom I've gained from my field, to provide a much-needed stimulus to the world and drive new change. When viewed through the lens of an open system, I was able to discover many new and interesting facts in history.

As current world history attests, renowned universities and prestigious organizations have always been open societies. A group that acknowledges the physical limitations of the conditions surrounding it, such as the world, the mind, and material resources, while also opening up its closed boundaries to communication, has evolved positively and grown into a prestigious institution.

While I cannot say with 100% scientific certainty, my qualitative conclusion is that an open attitude leads the world and enables open innovation through convergence and integration. To reiterate, the key is an open mind. When you open your mind, innovation follows

As mentioned earlier, history provides numerous examples of

people who embraced innovation with an open mind. The Silhak (實學) intellectual movement of the 17th and 18th centuries exemplifies this open system. The idea that Koreans could learn from those considered "barbarians" by traditional Confucian scholars was truly revolutionary. The Silhak scholars' (實學派) desire to learn with an open mind and innovate for practical life remains a valuable lesson today.

21st century Korea needs a new generation of Silhak scholars. Whether it be individuals, groups, the government, foreign relations, the North Korean issue, or any other field, we desperately need people with an open mindset. We urgently need open-minded individuals who can transcend the boundaries of science and humanities and pursue their dreams beyond national borders. Through this 'Open System' project, I hope to bring together new trends of convergence, fusion, and integration, enabling individuals to surpass conventional wisdom and limitations, and actively contribute throughout South Korea.

Hope is the exclusive possession of those who open their hearts. Open innovation is a gift reserved for those who open their minds. Therefore, young people of Korea, let us open up, expand our horizons, and embrace new ideas. Let us open our hearts wide and take a deep breath. And let us take a giant step forward. I wish all those who are making progress in the face of great difficulties great glory.

Embrace the 'Open System' project and all it offers!